ALSO BY THE AUTHOR

Heralding Article 25: A people's strategy for world transformation

Towards a universal basic income for all humanity

The intersection of politics and spirituality in addressing the climate crisis

Studies on the principle of sharing

The commons of humanity

The sharing economy

Inaugurating an Age of the Heart

Mohammed Sofiane Mesbahi

Matador
Unit E2 Airfield Business Park,
Harrison Road, Market Harborough,
Leicestershire. LE16 7UL
Tel: 0116 2792299
Email: books@troubador.co.uk
Web: www.troubador.co.uk/matador
Twitter: @matadorbooks

ISBN 978 1803130 583

British Library Cataloguing in Publication Data.
A catalogue record for this book is available from the British Library.

Typeset in 11pt Adobe Garamond Pro by Troubador Publishing Ltd, Leicester, UK

Matador is an imprint of Troubador Publishing Ltd

*"Morally it makes no difference whether a human
being is killed in war or is condemned to starve
to death because of the indifference of others."*

– Willy Brandt
(Chancellor of Germany from 1969-1974)

Contents

Editor's preface

As this book is printed in late 2021, five years after it was originally published online at sharing.org, it is interesting to observe how excitement for the idea of a sharing economy has significantly diminished. The term was always ambiguous, with widely differing interpretations of its authentic meaning. Much of the general public today are still likely to understand a sharing economy in its traditional and communal sense, as people freely sharing possessions among one another, or voluntarily helping the less fortunate in society. At the same time, many modern proponents of sharing remain enthusiastic about the development of peer-to-peer technologies to transform human relationships and address urgent social problems.

It was never the author's intention to directly engage with this nouveaux sharing movement, or to critique its sudden evolution in the post-financial crash years. However, it is notable that the predictions made in the first chapter have turned out to be prescient. The new business ventures of the profit-driven sharing economy have made millions for their investors, but have they done anything to raise public consciousness about the world's escalating human and environmental emergencies? Is it not, therefore, inevitable that these commercialised forms of interpersonal sharing should eventually 'collapse and become redundant in the longer term'?

Yet the truly moral and political idea of a sharing economy retains the utmost relevance for our lives in the twenty-first century. From the author's perspective as the founder of Share The World's Resources (STWR), that idea has always belonged to the poor, especially those who suffer from acute malnutrition and other severe material deprivations. And it is an idea that should always have been directed towards our governments, not only nationally but also globally through the United Nations in order to end poverty, conflict and ecological destruction. The real social movement for sharing is therefore grounded in the strenuous pursuit of justice and human rights, and it consists of all those who are struggling to reorder the world's priorities on behalf of the greater common good.

This simple understanding of a sharing economy is, sadly, still far from reaching a mainstream audience. But Mohammed Mesbahi goes much further in contemplating the inner or spiritual dimensions of the principle of sharing, which points to its most long-lasting and inwardly transformative implications. We are consequently led to ponder the significance of a new spiritual education based on the Art of Being and Self-realisation, as reflected in the Ageless Wisdom teachings that have been released to humanity over millennia.

Such a line of enquiry comprises the highest interpretation of a sharing economy whose time is yet to come. Hopefully it won't be long until people everywhere embrace this pioneering vision, and so begin the hard work of transforming our tragically divided world.

London, UK, June 2021

PART I

What does it mean to 'share'?

*The energy that we call love has always been here to
guide us within our personal lives and throughout
our spiritual evolution. But life after life we have
tended to look in the other direction, which
has ever written the sad and painful history
of our dysfunctional civilisation.*

What is the sharing economy, and what is its meaning and significance for the world we live in today? If you try and investigate this question through the internet, there are many debates and misleading definitions that you will soon come across. The sharing economy is commonly understood as a rising phenomenon of the new millennium that leverages information technology through peer-to-peer platforms, empowering individuals to share goods and services through bartering, leasing or the swapping of private assets. There is also a revival of non-monetised initiatives under this broad umbrella which enable communities to share more in their daily lives, whether it's through informal groups that come together with a common aim and purpose, or cooperative endeavours that provide shared access to skills, time, knowledge and productive spaces. Despite some controversies that have dogged the most popular initiatives in recent years, many of their leading advocates continue to espouse an idealistic vision of how the sharing economy can help to catalyse a social transition towards a more egalitarian, participatory and environmentally sustainable world.[1]

But are these technology-driven innovations really the sum total of what it means to 'share' in modern societies? And is it true that the sharing economy is still in its infancy today, as is so often stated by those who comment on this fast expanding trend? The fact is that sharing has always been with us as a distinctly human characteristic, and even applies to the sub-human kingdoms of nature as well as to the higher spiritual realms that are much hypothesised in esoteric philosophy. We have always shared within our homes and peer groups without the need for smartphones and high technology. This would include the sharing of food, possessions and the other basic necessities of life, as well as the living space, conviviality and mutual support that is fundamental to our health and prosperity. We share the common lands with our neighbours and communities. We share the roads, the public transport, the air and nature that surrounds us. Our human civilisations would never have survived since the first known hominins unless we practised sharing on an interpersonal and communal basis. It is, indeed, an evolutionary trait that behavioural scientists and anthropologists have long recognised as intrinsic to our essential nature.[2]

It is also a trait that is necessarily expressed, however incipiently or insufficiently, on both national and global levels through appropriate government activity on behalf of the common good. The Roman Empire is renowned for institutionalising many forms of economic sharing, for example, while the contemporary welfare state has its roots in the social insurance schemes introduced by Bismarck in Germany during the 1880s. The National Health Service created by the United Kingdom in the 1940s is perhaps a foremost example in modern history of a sharing economy that exists to protect all citizens from the insecurities of life, as similarly established across Western Europe and other industrialised nations in its various forms. Of the many different levels and modes of sharing within nations, the ideal of universality in social protection through redistributive policies is, arguably, the most practical expression of economic sharing that humanity has yet realised.[3]

But not everyone would agree with this simple observation. In our day, the founding principles of such publicly-funded systems—concerning equality of opportunity, the equitable distribution of wealth, and the collective responsibility for securing everyone's basic human rights—are increasingly being jeopardised by the market orientation of our societies. And as we shall broadly elucidate, the worldwide implementation of these core principles through intergovernmental cooperation is far from a reality in the early 21st century, regardless of the rapid process of international economic integration over recent decades.[4] Nonetheless, it remains a fact that the sharing economy has always been with us in one form or another. It should be obvious that sharing has forever played its part in our everyday lives, however long we have managed to avoid its crucial manifestation as a principle that underpins our global economic system. Only now, it appears, are we suddenly becoming aware of the importance of sharing and cooperation as the keystone of economic life, even if that understanding has been largely limited to the emerging forms of collaboration in commercial spheres.

To be sure, these new social activities based on access to rather than ownership of resources are still in their infancy, although they are really the revival of ancient practices of social interrelationship that are now being facilitated by modern business methods and advanced computer technologies. The underlying mode of interaction is comparable to much earlier human civilisations, except that everything is now happening so much faster than before, and through such digitalised and sophisticated techniques, that it gives rise to the illusion of being completely original. There is also a curious relationship to be observed between the advancing technologies of recent decades and the seemingly rapid passing of time. This has further given rise to the sense that society is evolving very quickly, and that we are even approaching a new era in which sharing could become the defining modus operandi in economic and social affairs. That impression may well prove to be true, but have we properly understood what sharing means for the world as a whole, however earnestly we may be responding to this visionary thoughtform that is everywhere pervading human consciousness?

*

Before we add the word 'economy' to the word 'sharing', we should first ponder the human value of sharing per se in the context of this unfortunate planet in which the forces of commercialisation are creating such havoc and devastation. If we are seriously interested in investigating what sharing means in relation to world problems, we must start from the awareness that rampant commercialisation is the greatest danger facing humanity today, based as it is on the opposite propensities to sharing in both its theoretical and literal meaning.[5] This may sound like a rather elementary observation, but how can you have a viable sharing economy in a world that is so unequal as a result of centuries of colonialism, imperialism and laissez-faire

8

globalisation, leading to such discrepancies in living standards within and between different countries?[6] Yet few sharing economy advocates appear to begin from this fundamental standpoint, which is to perceive the urgent necessity of sharing the world's resources as an antidote to the enduring crime of widespread penury amidst plenty.

Perhaps you believe that the prevalence of poverty is steadily improving, and as such it is an issue that can be left to our governments to resolve. After all, most leading politicians and business executives continue to propagate such a message during high-profile conferences, like the annual World Economic Forum in Davos.[7] Even some aid and development organisations have fallen into the trap of believing the myth that rising prosperity for the few will eventually benefit the majority, notwithstanding the visible evidence of widening inequalities of wealth and income on an unprecedented scale.

Heads of state may have vowed to end all forms of poverty by 2030, as recently enshrined in the United Nation's Post-2015 Development Agenda.[8] But it's not difficult to perceive the fallacy of such promises while governments remain subject to the 'commercialisation paradigm', as we have discussed elsewhere.[9] That is to say, a prevailing political context in which the excessive influence of major corporations over government policymaking decisions makes it almost impossible to conceive of States committing to the international arrangements necessary to respect, protect and fulfil every individual's established socio-economic rights. The moment there is another global financial crisis, as widely anticipated, do we really believe that the dire hardships of the poorest individuals will be immediately prioritised by our existing government administrations? And do we believe that the noble elites who gather in Davos will make any less profits in their business dealings, even if the extreme poverty rate drastically surges?

One might presume that these are the kind of political and moral questions to ask oneself, if we are truly concerned about seeing the principle of sharing implemented as a global process that can meet the common needs of all people in all countries. But unfortunately, the sharing economy as presently understood is not remotely born of the awareness that humanity must share its resources more equitably in response to multiple converging crises, and on the basis of a civilisational emergency. It seems that the sharing economy today is predominantly related to commercial activity, to a vaguely collectivistic notion of accessing profitable amenities, but not to the awareness that we must share the bounteous produce of this earth if humanity is to survive. It is certainly not related to the idea of helping the world's hungry and destitute, the three billion people or more who suffer from undernourishment and other severe poverty-related deprivations.[10]

Even those who espouse the sharing economy's environmental benefits are not rightly concerned with the meaning of sharing in relation to the critical world situation. Consider the arguments that car sharing will mean there are less cars on the road, or that tool sharing libraries will mean less new products are purchased by individuals in affluent communities. Such a case may be empirically validated, but if that is the extent of our thinking on sharing then we are still trapped within the conditioning or 'ism' of consumerism, and limiting our awareness to the idea of 'consuming less', which has nothing to do with the sharing economy as properly envisioned and universally expressed. We should be careful to perceive how commercialisation hides in those new technologies, and how it makes us blind to the forces that condition us to buy and endlessly consume expensive merchandise, while we remain indifferent to the greater environmental and social problems all around us.

Possibly 90 percent of the supposed sharing economy is associated with commercial profit-making and self-interest to some degree, regardless of any positive social effects that may result from the usage of these cooperative internet platforms. Are we really convinced that this is where the true meaning of sharing is to be found, in accordance with its deepest philosophical and spiritual connotations? What we have really created is a new method for comfortable living, although that method is so constrained by money-making incentives that it is better described as a gentler form of commercialisation. The human mind loves to create new methods and 'isms', like the priest who believes in a particular conception of God, and then goes to study in a seminary that God which his own thinking has created. Without being aware of our mental conditioning and social conformity, the sharing economy advocate is sadly the same in promoting a more convenient and enjoyable way of life within an unsustainable, grossly unjust and increasingly unequal society that has no meaningful connection to the spiritual reality of our interdependent lives.

Thus instead of directing our sharing economy idea towards an emancipatory conception of justice and human rights, we continue to lower ourselves to the same level of consciousness as the corporate marketer who convinces us to 'buy one and get one for free'. There may be nothing wrong with promoting the ideas of collaborative consumption or shared ownership for budding entrepreneurs, but let's not pretend that we have reinvented the principle of sharing for the greatest good of the greatest number. In psychological terms it should be understood, at best, as a less stressful mode of living for the more privileged.

To look at the nature of sharing in its profoundest spiritual aspects, it may be discerned that the above-mentioned forms of interpersonal sharing are associated with the personality or lower self, which is a meagre reflection of the higher level of soul awareness that is conscious of the inherent unity and interconnectedness of humanity as a whole. We are all capable of realising this higher awareness that lies dormant and ever-present within us, however much it is suppressed by solely focusing our energies on what makes us feel comfortable and emotionally undisturbed within the little boxes of our social lives.

If you try and talk to someone whose energies are preoccupied with the lower personalised forms of sharing and collaboration, they will surely not be interested in listening to your case for sharing planetary resources between the governments of all nations to irrevocably end poverty, conflict and environmental destruction. Despite a deeper awareness of sharing lying dormant within them, they will refuse to look at it and unconsciously reject its transformative implications, because they feel more comfortable with the easy idea of sharing personal belongings within a local community. Yet the economic implementation of the principle of sharing is unlikely to be a comfortable experience at first, for there is so much work to be done, and so many oppositional forces that must be confronted in business and political spheres. Without a doubt, those powerful forces will eventually disturb us in our self-absorbed lives and well-intentioned endeavours. It will not be long until we are pushed, one way or another, to awaken to the necessity of transforming society as the world's crises prolong and climax in coming years.

The true vision of a sharing economy represents the end of the old ways defined by the pursuit of profit and competitive self-interest, while a new age of global cooperation can only begin through the channel of ending hunger in a world of such material and financial abundance. For now, the sharing economy begins with the poor, belongs to the poor, and remains beholden to the poor from any moral or real-world perspective. It will never begin from a petty notion of enhancing the convenience of our everyday lives. And as long as the idea of sharing is reduced to such a complacent and self-referential understanding, it will inevitably collapse and become redundant in the longer term. In the meantime, however, there may be lots of opportunities for making money under the commercialised banner of sharing, if that is our primary concern. How convenient indeed!

There is nothing to stop us from capitalising on the new sharing technologies and so-called disruptive business models, but we should at least try to be aware of and honest about our underlying motives and psychological attitudes. Are we really thinking about others and the state of the world as we carry on with our consumer-driven sharing behaviours? Or is it all about ourselves once again? Please look very closely at the sharing economy initiatives that have so far arisen throughout the Western world, and ask yourself if they have anything to do with the inner faculties of spiritual awareness that exemplify love, right relationship and the highest intelligence of man.

*

Most of the sharing advocates of today are pursuing the easiest and least stressful mode of human relations in affluent society, compared to the millions of marginalised people who are fighting for justice in poorer countries by sacrificing their blood, their freedom, their families and often their lives. That is the hard-core way of sharing, the real and toilsome path that is witnessed through the struggles of dispossessed indigenous peoples in India, the Palestinians in Gaza, the landless labourers in South America, the shack-dwellers and smallholder farmers in sub-Saharan Africa, the exploited garment workers in special economic zones across Asia, and so many others. All of the world's downtrodden masses are crying, however invisibly, for their government to implement a sharing economy that fulfils their most basic human rights.

Many popular uprisings are also indirectly calling for a sharing economy to be instituted through more inclusive and redistributive government policies. This includes the Arab Spring wave of demonstrations that aimed at deposing corrupt political regimes, as well as the anti-austerity demonstrations and Occupy movements that have mobilised in the name of increased social and economic equality.[11] We can perceive for ourselves how all these diverse protest activities are the manifestation of a growing call for sharing, even if that call is unconsciously expressed through a raw response to the injustice that stems from the imposition of an unfair economic system. To stand up for justice in a world that is characterised by growing inequalities and economic precariousness for the majority is inevitably a stressful undertaking. So it is understandable that the word 'sharing' is not on the lips of those activists who oppose the major corporations with their exploitative and profit-seeking activities, as well as the governments who uphold the interests of those powerful bastions of privilege and wealth.

Observe, also, the frontline servers of humanity within groups like the Red Cross or Médecins Sans Frontières. Together, they demonstrate the most human expression of the terms 'sharing' and 'economy' by working ceaselessly to assist neglected citizens in war-torn and impoverished regions, irrespective of caste, creed or race. There are many unrewarded heroes of a sharing economy, in this respect, who inadvertently define the sincerest meaning of sharing in their advocacy work and plans for world reconstruction. The list is long and familiar, comprising as it does the myriad grassroots activists, civil society organisations, and political campaigning networks who seek a more just and ecologically sustainable form of development. These committed individuals may not recognise the interrelation of their fight for justice with the explicit need for economic sharing, but the connection is palpable and real for anyone who perceives the problem of our dysfunctional societies with a compassionate awareness of the whole.

How closely, then, are the commercialised sharing initiatives of today aligned with these great social struggles and peoples' movements? None of the sharing economy practitioners in community-level movements appear to be interested in dedicating their efforts towards urging political leaders to share each nation's surplus wealth and resources on behalf of the subjugated poor. Not even, that is, to prevent the deaths of circa 40,000 people who die prematurely each day from poverty-related causes, often from malnutrition and childhood diseases that are barely witnessed in more affluent countries.[12] If that becomes our heartfelt and motivating concern, and not the comfort or convenience of our privileged lives within our communities, then perhaps we can rightfully identify ourselves as an ambassador for humanity through the principle of sharing. But if our idea of sharing remains limited to the confines of our own neighbourhood or social peer group, then we clearly have no idea what sharing can achieve as the royal road towards environmental sustainability, peace and justice.

There are innumerable communities around the world that have attempted to share among themselves and achieve a more harmonious and sustainable way of life. But perhaps it is time to ask ourselves what good such communities can achieve when the world's ecological crises are rapidly reaching the point of no return. While manifold spiritual communes and eco-villages have long emerged and then disbanded in the fullness of time, the intensifying trends of commercialisation over recent decades may eventually end all possibilities of achieving a self-sustaining community idyll. Indeed, how long can these trends remain left unchecked in a world that is becoming irremediably divided and environmentally degraded?

This is not to decry the countless grassroots initiatives that aim to reduce individual carbon footprints within modern societies by conserving the earth's natural resources. Many provide invaluable models for how to shift towards sustainable modes of food production, housing, transport, energy generation and so on. The ethics of sharing and sufficiency on a small and local scale may soon become the watchwords of our time, as long recognised by sustainability practitioners in various fields. Yet even these pioneers of community resilience often fail to mention the words 'poverty' or 'hunger' in their literature and ideas. Does this mean they are empowered with an awareness of the whole, and immersed in the human reality of the critical world situation? To believe we can find peace by retreating to a remote community is still a fantasy, no matter how frugal or self-sustaining our lifestyles, for the civilisational crisis we face is spiritual in its origins and the outcome of millennia of destructive human behaviours. Throughout our ancestry and our many past incarnations, we have all played a part in repeating the gross injustices and divisions that are passed down from generation to generation. The intention of leading a peaceful, secluded and sustainable way of life amidst all the turmoil of these times is therefore to divide oneself from the inherent unity of the human race, unless we also contribute our energies towards creating a more equal world in which everyone has their basic needs fulfilled. That spiritual understanding, that inner realisation, and that motivating ideal is the only real peace we can experience within ourselves at this perilous juncture in history. For then we are not alone in the struggle for a world that 'shares' in any meaningful sense of that term.

What does this mean for the modern sharing advocates whose intentions remain knowingly or unknowingly overshadowed by commercialisation, and who have already undignified the principle of sharing with their mental blindness and concern for moneymaking? To be interested in the sharing economy without any concern for the dire suffering of others means that your ideas are merely created by habitual thoughts, and without connecting to the inner awareness of the heart. Hence you will only succeed in reducing a profoundly human and spiritual conception into another 'ism' that has no relationship to the real nature of justice, balance or the oneness of humanity. Out of your desire to create and enjoy a new method for comfortable living, you will inadvertently abduct the principle of sharing for your own self-interested pursuits, until 'shareism' becomes the norm.

Is that not already the case, and should not the proponents of sharing in its many commercialised forms be ashamed of themselves? With the obvious knowledge that extreme poverty is still rampant on this earth, how is it possible that the idea of sharing is not directed towards saving our brothers and sisters who are dying from preventable diseases, starvation, wars and climate disasters? What makes man so blind, so poor within and indifferent to the one Life that surrounds him? Why does he limit his awareness to his community, to his new innovations and his fragmented way of living by continuously being attached to his indifference—an indifference that dismisses the wisdom and the many silent cries of his heart? What makes man so small, so trapped and confused within the mechanism of his vain ideations, when he is so free, so great within the very presence of his own soul—a soul with a divine purpose that says LOVE ALL and SACRIFICE FOR ALL THAT LIVES…?

*

To pursue the idea and praxis of sharing within the paradigm of commercialisation is futile in the end, for these two distinct processes are antithetical in both their inner and outer expression. As we have previously observed, one is divisive in its complexity, while the other is unifying in its simplicity.[13] One is manipulative, amoral and harmful towards both man and the lower kingdoms of nature, while the other is predicated on fairness, harmlessness, awareness and the will-to-good. The wider economic expression of sharing even exemplifies love and the profoundest understanding of compassion which our present-day culture has again degraded into its lowermost and often sentimental meaning. Surely the thoughtform of a sharing economy will evolve into a more moral and inclusive idea over time. But as long as it is not grounded in a political conception of justice for the world's poor, then it is certain that a transformative vision of sharing resources between governments will remain in its infancy for many, many years to come.

There are an increasing number of intellectuals who are now beginning to engage with the authentic meaning of sharing as a new economic and political paradigm.[14] While it is an encouraging sign that many able thinkers are examining such concepts as 'fair shares', 'the commons' and 'degrowth' through an academic lens, what do these scholarly definitions achieve for the poorest people who are desperately asking their governments to share a measly portion of the nation's wealth, just so they and their family can eat a square meal each day? That modest plea from an impoverished person is the embodiment of a sharing economy in all its purity and essence, so how does the well-fed intellectual often overlook this simple truth? Few appear to acknowledge the fact that millions of innocent lives could be saved each year, if only the plentiful resources of this world were adequately shared. The call for sharing in its manifold forms is invariably an expression of common sense, yet it is possible to respond to common sense in an overly cerebral manner that can exclude the less educated citizens and eventually confuse, misguide and entangle us in endless hypothetical debates about the right path forwards. For this reason again, any investigation into the meaning of a sharing economy must begin with a preliminary understanding that chronic undernourishment must be effaced from this earth as a leading societal and political priority. As long as we start from this fundamental standpoint, our inspired analyses and policy proposals cannot go too far astray.

Consider the example of those physicians working for Médecins Sans Frontières who would like to see an end to the insanity of war, but first they must deal with the reality that thousands of people in conflict zones are being neglected by their governments, and are thus in need of life-saving medical attention that is sorely lacking in this sorrowful world. By analogy, the intellectual idea of sharing within modern societies is important to debate and hypothesise, but first we must redirect our attention to the millions of people in poorer countries who continue to suffer from severe deprivations without any form of government welfare or public support.

Try to contemplate the inner relationship you may have between your own daily concerns in a relatively privileged and comfortable household, and the reality of life for a person who is at this moment dying from a preventable disease or malnutrition. Your heartfelt awareness about the lives of those who are less fortunate than yourself, and your private intention to do something to help end this spiritual blasphemy in our midst—that awareness is, in itself, an awareness of the need for a sharing economy to be instituted across the world. Any act that tries to contribute towards ending the prevalent suffering caused by absolute poverty is, in itself, the purest expression of a sharing economy via the heart, via our maturity and via common sense, especially if that act is focused on trying to persuade our political representatives to commit to sharing the resources of the world.

Have you ever held someone in your arms who is dying from malnutrition in a poor region such as sub-Saharan Africa, knowing that back home your family and friends are able to access adequate food, shelter, healthcare and other necessities as a basic human right? Following that profound and tragic experience, it is assured that your understanding of the sharing economy will assume a very different resonance and meaning within your heart and mind, and it is very unlikely to be directed solely towards oneself and one's more advantaged social peer group.

Consider also the person who loses a dearly beloved family member from an incurable disease or tragedy. As a consequence of that sad event, they may suddenly transform their life purpose by dedicating time and energy to preventing others from befalling a similar fate, such as by creating a charitable organisation or campaigning for social change. Thus that individual's awareness and empathy has been markedly expanded, while their erstwhile complacency has completely vanished. Such is the hope for the sharing economy idea—and on a scale that is inconceivable—if the millions of people who enjoy an adequate standard of living can together expand their empathic awareness to include the needless deprivations experienced by the poorer two-thirds majority of the world population.

We are not trying to contemplate the deeper philosophical meaning of compassion in these sparse analogies, but simply trying to observe, in straightforward human terms, the need for greater awareness in our societies through the common sense that arises from an engaged heart. It not only concerns the need to end the appalling reality of hunger and life-threatening poverty; it is also about love in the most general and pragmatic sense, as expressed in a civilised and moral attitude to life that cares about the needless suffering of others. The present author has discussed before the meaning of love from a basically spiritual and psychological perspective, which is a motivating energy that can bring about the total reorientation of a person's life pursuits once an awareness of the heart determines one's inner attitudes and behaviours.[15]

We can observe the psychological and spiritual transformation of an individual via the awakening of the heart in almost every department of human activity, and the misguided advocates of commercialised forms of economic sharing are no exception. All we can hope is that the self-proclaimed sharers of today will become aware of how they are degrading the higher meanings of this misapplied principle, and hence change their ways by joining with the millions of others who are valiantly fighting for a just world that permits no-one to suffer or die from a lack of access to life's essentials.

PART II

From the inner to the outer sharing economy

Article 25 is one of the outer expressions of the principle of sharing, and spiritual evolution is the inner expression of that very principle.

Now let us turn our attention towards the inner meaning of a sharing economy, bearing in mind that we cannot propose a glossary definition from a spiritual or psychological perspective, for the meaning of sharing stems from the heart and not from intellectual activity alone. Even at the lowest understanding of sharing in personal terms as discussed above, we are unlikely to comprehend the real significance of its potential until our thoughts are directed by the heart at all times. Let the heart be the architect of our sharing economy that we build with awareness and love, otherwise it will never bring about the better world we yearn for. We have tried everything else over thousands of years, throughout all the epochs and civilisations that have proudly arisen and long since disappeared; all we have left is love and the heart! But how will we know when humanity is embracing the inner meaning of a sharing economy through the awareness of an engaged heart? Allow me to reaffirm: it will not be until a huge swathe of the world population comes together and passionately declares their heartfelt determination to see an end to all forms of poverty everywhere, for once and for all.

Such words are easy to express but far more difficult to conceive as a reality in the everyday awareness of countless millions of people. How, then, can we perceive the inwardly transformative aspects of the sharing economy, when it requires us to have a holistic view of the world that is seldom evidenced in our present-day social and cultural ideations? We may begin by contemplating the preceding chapter before going within ourselves to quietly reflect on the deeper meaning of sharing in our divided world. Through our intuition, perhaps we will both perceive and feel the emotional significance of what is being conveyed in these insufficient words.

Compassion in the highest spiritual sense means an impersonal awareness of the good of the whole, not only the particular. Hence there is no evidence of selfless compassion in an awareness that is limited to the good of any single person, family, community or nation. It is by no means a wrongdoing if our awareness is generally preoccupied with the good of our own particular neighbourhood or society. But if we want to perceive the holistic meaning of a sharing economy then we must also expand our empathic concerns to the needs of the world in its entirety—which requires us to embrace a vision of the one Humanity with absolute sincerity, honesty and maturity. We may care for our own communities first, although we must also turn our attention outwards—as if, for example, I am called to feed my own neighbour who is hungry, before I look out towards the world to see that everyone else has their basic needs secured.

A spiritual and holistic understanding of the sharing economy therefore means that we are no longer dividing ourselves from the rest of humanity, either inwardly or outwardly. In this sense, the inner meaning of sharing is far removed from any systematic method of exchanging commoditised goods or services; it means 'to be with' in all respects—compassionately, morally, ethically and lovingly. It means to have awareness of the existence and purpose of the soul, which is an esoteric reality that we have yet to comprehend with all its immense implications for our materialistic and commercialised cultures. It also means 'not to harm', for there is invariably harmfulness in the opposite propensities to sharing that result in social division and conflict, as principally defined by our greed, selfishness, hatred, and above all our complacency and indifference.

Most of us are so conditioned by the norms of our dysfunctional societies that we are completely blind to these simple truths, leaving us with no understanding of the extraordinary versatility of the principle of sharing and its import for our spiritual evolution. Thus the idea of a sharing economy is far, far greater than we can presently envision. If we employ a metaphor of an architect who builds forms with material substance, the true innovators of a sharing economy are like architects tasked with building new forms through the energy of love. For indeed, the primary significance of sharing is its evidence of the existence of love—a love that means you give and want nothing back in return. Like the inspired architect wants his buildings to be recognised worldwide, so should we want this expanded idea of a sharing economy to be globalised into everyone's hearts. We need to both import and export our love to every country, let us say. And in today's divided world, the only way to achieve that loving objective is by universalising our demand for an irrevocable end to poverty-induced hunger.

Reflecting on the above commentary may help us to better grasp how the sharing economy has almost no relation to the social activities and market transactions that currently define its meaning. Rather, it should be rooted in an awareness of the reality of the inner self, which would signify the spark of something entirely new on this earth that presages a psychological revolution within the consciousness of humanity. It can also be construed that the moral or spiritual idea of a sharing economy has been with us for millennia, as embodied within many esoteric and religious doctrines and reflected in a symbolical interpretation of the Christ Principle. To borrow from the Christian phraseology, the spiritual significance of sharing is its ability to lead us to an awareness of the Christ within our hearts. This is in sharp contrast to the simplistic view of sharing in a modern commercialised society that leads to nowhere and nothing except for one's own comfort, convenience and temporary emotional satisfaction.

Such an interpretation lends a further spiritual justification to our assertion that the principle of sharing belongs firstly to the poor and thus resides in the inner heart awareness that dwells within each and every individual, as variously expressed in all the ancient scriptures and teachings on right human relations. To be sure, the spiritual verity of sharing has never belonged to a self-regarding notion of social wellbeing that is pursued as if the millions of hungry people across the world did not exist; as if the huge surpluses of food stocks and other essential commodities did not exist; as if the technology and manpower did not exist to transport these indispensable resources to where they are most critically needed.

So there is a marked difference between the meaning of sharing as an accustomed practice between people in their everyday lives, and the divine principle of sharing that can only be understood through the intelligence of an awakened heart and mind. If we were able to raise our consciousness in meditation and properly tune with the principle of sharing as a divine conception, all we would see upon opening our eyes to the world is injustice in every direction, and an unfathomable indifference that allows millions of people to die like flies from hunger while food is left rotting elsewhere and wasted in colossal amounts. Yet we cannot save these defenceless victims from our indifference unless our governments implement the principle of sharing on a multilateral scale. We need a massive international relief effort to provide for adequate housing, health and medical care, clean water and sanitation, financial transfers and everything else the poor in less developed countries need to live with dignity and economic security. Only then can we talk about the true beginnings of a sharing economy as the guiding light of global social policy and international development.

We would do well, in this regard, to refer to the Brandt Commission Report of 1980 to garner a broad indication of what it means to share the world's resources through a comprehensive multilateral plan of action.[16] That is where the loving, compassionate and mature vision of the sharing economy is to be found. We are mainly referring to the concept of an emergency programme of poverty eradication and economic reform that must be structured through the United Nations, which represents the best hope we have for administering a global system of resource sharing on a permanent and structural basis. Just as governments see the United Nations as an appropriate international body to decide whether or not they should go to war (however ignoble their political motives), it is also the only multilateral institution in existence that can viably represent the common interests of all its member states in reshaping global North-South relations. After all, it was the founding of the United Nations that created both the possibility and hope for a more equitable world order after the Second World War. Despite the need for considerable reform and democratisation of the United Nations system, there is no gainsaying its potential for coordinating the immense process of redistributing aid and surplus resources to foreseeably end extreme human deprivation within a short span of years.[17]

In sum, we can conclude that the idea of a sharing economy must be universal in its application; it must be predicated on the concern for right distribution as opposed to maximum profitmaking through economic competition; and it must incorporate the principle of giving without seeking anything in return—all of which must be envisioned in terms of a free circulation of essential commodities between nations under a democratised system of global governance.

None of this bears much relation to our existing theories and practices of international aid. This is grossly inadequate in its present form and often transferred with conditionalities that primarily benefit multinational corporations or the competitive interests of donor nations. Only secondarily (and often very selectively) does overseas development assistance provide the means for less developed countries to redistribute wealth and improve the lives of their poor majority of citizens, which any political campaigning group will corroborate in painstaking detail.[18]

Can we hereby stretch our imaginations sufficiently to envision a world in which governments fulfil their responsibilities to guarantee all people an adequate standard of living, as long enshrined in international human rights law? A world in which the role of NGOs and charities in relieving human suffering is eventually surpassed by the actions of our coordinated governments working through the United Nations, whether in response to life-threatening poverty, conflict, natural disasters or forced migration in any form? A world in which Article 25 of the Universal Declaration of Human Rights is finally guaranteed for every man, woman and child without exception, thus signifying the merest beginnings of a sharing economy that moves in the right direction at long last?[19]

The prospect of consummating this vision may not seem too radical or utopian, when we also consider the sheer amount of financial capital and wealth that is circulating around the world, and the comparatively negligible sums that are needed to lift everyone out of poverty.[20] Yet no such vision can be realised until a majority of the global public is dedicated to this epochal cause, and continually presses every leading politician to put an end to poverty-related suffering as their first and last concern. Can we expect a sharing economy to be established by political elites taking action at their own behest when the forces of commercialisation are still dictating the agenda of any politician who comes to power, and ever more so by the day? Or do we believe that billionaire corporate philanthropists can solve the world's problems on our behalf, without the need for ordinary people to transform society by engaging with the attributes of their hearts?

Observe very carefully the actions and intentions of major donors to charities and non-governmental organisations, who often purport to be the heroic saviours of the poor by committing large sums of money to their chosen cause. Even if the outcome of their contribution is to achieve some relative good for those fortunate recipients, it still has no relation to either the inner meaning of a sharing economy in terms of our spiritual unity and interrelatedness, or the outer meaning of sharing world resources that must be structured by governments through new economic arrangements and a significantly reformed and re-empowered United Nations.

Suppose a wealthy philanthropist became infused with a compassionate awareness of the need to end the existence of poverty as if it were a civilisational emergency. Perhaps they would no longer be driven to make excessive profits from their commercial pursuits, instead committing their time and personal wealth to the cause of realising a cooperative sharing economy among the comity of nations. Perhaps they would help build a global network of impassioned activists, recognising that this is the necessary means for persuading our governments to reorder their priorities and bring a measure of peace and justice to the world.

May this last thought spark our imagination about what a worldwide show of support for a sharing economy might look like—built upon an alliance of every public-spirited civil society organisation, and backed by the concerted will of innumerable people from every walk of life. Thus shall be the real social movement for sharing in all its consummated glory, as characterised and animated by an explosion of joy across the world, and as recognised by its service to the most disempowered and neglected individuals. Thus shall it be, and thus shall we know that divinity has manifested again in a physical form, when millions upon millions of people uphold Article 25 as a shining beacon for the rehabilitation of our world.[21]

*

There is much more to discuss and consider as we postulate what a sharing economy signifies in the broadest terms, and it is important to recognise that our awareness of its meaning will gradually change and evolve as the whole architecture of the global economic system is restructured. We have contemplated how the first stage involves an enormous number of people worldwide calling on their governments to redistribute resources towards the hungry and the neglected poor, those who have insufficient access to the basic necessities of life. That may be considered the most primal expression of sharing as a global process that is gradually systematised through the construction of a just world economic order. And that is when the reality of a sharing economy will begin to reveal itself through new modes of global governance and transformed structures of trade and finance, well beyond the recommendations proposed by the Brandt Commission in 1980 or any high-level report thereafter.[22]

Yet we cannot foresee an alternative global economic system that incorporates a process of resource sharing as its basic operating principle, while we continue to suffer from the effects of a corrupt, divisive and unbalanced system that functions in the opposite direction. As much as the Security Council has to be decommissioned before we can envision the great future destiny of the Assembly of Nations, the current economic system must be effectively dismantled before we can envision the anticipated structures based on genuine cooperation and economic sharing.[23] The theories and blueprints may well exist, as evidenced in the proposals of many forward-looking policy thinkers and civil society groups. But no-one can predict with exactitude the eventual appearance of an alternative system of global resource distribution in four or five decades time.

Suffice to say that over the past two thousand years, the highest aspiration of governments concerned the need to organise and advance the individuality of each nation on the competitive world stage, as encapsulated in conventional notions of state sovereignty. But as humanity comes of age, each nation is tasked with expanding that overly pronounced individuality to the international level in support of the good of the whole, which can only be achieved via the sharing of essential resources and a cultural orientation towards ideals of selfless service.

Hence the importance of the United Nations as new structures of global economic governance are gradually realised on the basis of trust and consensus, with each nation ultimately contributing their surplus resources to some form of global pool that is equitably redistributed on the basis of need and the common good, as opposed to purely commercial considerations or strategic national interests. Such is the quintessential vision of a sharing economy that can promote the interdependency of all nations as one village, while respecting and preserving the distinct identities of diverse populations with all their manifold cultures, racial groups, and religious and political persuasions.

For the reader who finds this vision too vague or lacking in technical details, the main point to reflect upon is that the outer meaning of a sharing economy will go through many stages of understanding in our awareness, since its development is intertwined with and dependent upon the gradual expansion of human consciousness. Again we must return to the inner dimensions of sharing, since the outer or systemic expression of the sharing economy is extremely vast and endlessly evolving over time. Indeed, its origins lie not in thoughts or policy prescriptions, but in the latent human faculty of spiritual awareness.

As we earlier intimated, the outer expression of the sharing economy in its final universal form is a reflection of our inner spiritual unity that is a basic truth on higher planes of being or consciousness—namely, that reality which is referred to in the Ageless Wisdom teachings as the Kingdom of Souls.[24] If we can accept this premise even as a working hypothesis, then the preceding thoughts may become much clearer in our minds and inspire us to enquire deeper into this subject for ourselves.

Hearken to the prospect of millions of people worldwide calling on governments to immediately prevent the shameless reality of needless poverty-related deaths. That unprecedented occurrence will represent the first major recognition of our inner spiritual unity on the outer physical plane, as represented by huge numbers of ordinary people uniting in peaceful protest on behalf of the good of the whole, of the one Humanity. Such a magnificent spectacle will also demonstrate the fact that a preliminary consensus exists among a significant proportion of the global public who demand a fairer sharing of planetary resources, and who realise this is our last hope of averting further social, economic and environmental catastrophe. Many shall disagree, no doubt, and many shall remain impassive or unmoved by the worsening trends of world crises. But the fact of a people's consensus on sharing the world's resources will be known as soon as governments are compelled to organise an emergency redistribution programme, thus to save the dying poor in their many hundreds of thousands as the jubilant months pass by.

The hearts of men and women everywhere are unconsciously ready for this consensus to reveal itself through the combined activities of those who unite on a single issue. The oppressed and neglected poor, likewise, have always been ready to lend their voice when the time comes. Then, and only then, will the call for sharing be recognised as a peaceful and implacable phenomenon with the power to determine the policies of the world's governments. Then everyone who participates in this cause of all causes, this movement of all movements, will know exactly what actions they should take as a subjectively unified group that is motivated by its concern for the critical needs of others.

What should be clear from these prognostications is that a fairer international economic system cannot be structured without the awareness of ordinary people to firstly embrace, and thereafter sustain its enduring implementation. This compels us to look at ourselves inwardly with an honest mind if we want to perceive an answer to the question that vexes every forward-looking political thinker: How can we bring about a definitive sharing economy that operates at the international level and fulfils the basic needs of all, while respecting environmental boundaries? For there can be no sharing economy that exists throughout the entire world, benefiting every family and individual in equal measure, until we have established a more joyful, participatory and trusting way of life in our respective societies. And there can be no alternative paradigm of sharing that exists within a less resource-constrained and overpopulated planet, until every person has the economic security and freedom that is needed to explore their inborn creative potential.

What's more, there can be no sharing economy idea that persists into the long distant future without the aforesaid ability of the majority populace to embrace an awareness of the whole, as well as the particular. An awareness that understands how urgent it is for humanity to live together with a sense of unity and oneness, free from the bane of penury and conflict. An awareness that guides each individual towards a simpler and more equitable standard of living, considering the severity of climate change and environmental degradation that is still far from the urgent preoccupations of most people in affluent societies.[25]

And if we ourselves can detect the first intimations of this new awareness beginning to develop within the vanguard of progressive thought and experimentation, then we may also begin to perceive the final destination where it is taking us—which is towards new modes of economic exchange and social relationships based on barter. Already, the loving expression of sharing on a community scale is reflected in contemporary notions of a gift economy, whereby the role of money as a medium of exchange is deprioritised in favour of the innate social tendency towards voluntary giving and receiving.[26] Thus allow your mind to intuitively grasp the social and cultural ramifications of implementing the principle of sharing on a worldwide basis, as encapsulated in our line of reasoning:

> » Firstly, through an emergency programme organised by governments working cooperatively through relevant international agencies to redistribute essential resources and ameliorate the prevalence of hunger and life-threatening poverty.
>
> » And secondly, through a restructured global economy that incorporates a systemic process of sharing natural resources and essential commodities as its fundamental operating principle, divorced from the profit motive and monopolistic private interests.

What do we foresee as the outcome of such inter-governmental economic arrangements that develop over many decades, where the predominant power of big banks and other financial institutions is progressively transferred to a democratically reformed and entrusted United Nations system? Logically, the idea and existence of a sharing economy will evolve into something much different over time that is conceivable as an advanced system of global bartering and exchange, for which we may need a new lexicon of the political economy to describe. This will not be barter as we think of it now, as a primitive form of reciprocal trade once characteristic of archaic societies. Let us try to visualise, instead, a complex system of global resource management that is administered with the use of massive information technologies and complex transportation logistics to maintain a sufficient, sustainable circulation of commonly-owned goods and resources among all nations.

Our concern here is not with the specific details of how these future economic arrangements may function. Undoubtedly, there are endless hypothetical questions to be answered about how we can achieve the universal and free distribution of essential resources, especially in relation to the great public utilities like energy and water. What is more important to consider at this time are the inner changes that humanity must undergo if these outer economic changes are to become a feasible reality. From this line of enquiry, it is necessary to perceive how the human propensity to express goodwill, joy, creativity and frugality is embedded within any new global economic system that integrates the principle of barter into its foundational mechanisms and institutional framework.

We can begin by thinking for ourselves, in simple terms, about how bartering among individuals on a widespread scale—if there is absolutely no money or profit involved—will lead to the simplification of wants and needs; a lessening of stress and greed; and the unleashing of greater freedom and inner creativity. Perhaps we can grasp a faint precognition of how this newfound realisation of trust and goodwill on an interpersonal basis will, automatically, facilitate the introduction of bartering as an economic system within different nations, in accordance with the particular approaches suited to each nation's unique circumstances, culture and traditions. To be sure, it is the social and economic process of bartering within nations that will facilitate and sustain the introduction of a global system of bartering among the world's governments. Then we may have finally reached a stage where humanity resembles a great colony of bees that cooperate for the good of the whole, with the United Nations representing our metaphorical queen.

Such an outcome would not have to signal a return to pre-capitalist models of trade and consumption. On the contrary, an economy guided by the forces of commercialisation through unbridled market competition is holding us back in our evolution, and predisposing the youth towards the pursuit of materialistic goals and self-centred ambitions. There is no reason why we cannot envisage an enduringly peaceful, equitable and sustainable world order that absorbs all the good of humanity's previous advancements in technology and science, yet also encompasses a process of free exchange of essential commodities as the bedrock of socio-economic relations. What's more, there is no reason to suppose that such a civilisation may not include a much relegated role for private enterprise and market competition in those areas of life that are unrelated to either the fulfilment of basic human needs, or the sustainable distribution of non-renewable resources.

If we can accept these general propositions, then we may agree that the way of sharing and voluntary simplicity is inseparably connected with the eventual introduction of an advanced system of bartering and exchange among the family of nations. The actions of governments cooperating to institute these new economic processes on an international basis will, necessarily, go hand-in-hand with similar processes being instituted across nations and within municipalities, communities and neighbourhoods. And through the confluence of these gradual transformations, enacted by both states and citizens of their own volition, we may finally witness the proof that humanity can live more simply and equally within the means of this bountiful earth.

Thus the greater meaning of a sharing economy can be summarised in the following terms: It shall represent the imminent end to an era defined by the dominance of material and commercial values. And in turn, it shall signify the resurrection of barter as the principle mode of economic exchange for the first time in modern history, albeit on a higher turn of the spiral that vouchsafes the continued spiritual evolution of our race.

PART III

A spiritual education for the Art of Being

The principle of sharing holds within itself not only the Art of Living, but also the Art of Being and Becoming.

*The Science of the Soul is your inheritance…
know yourself, then.*

And thus know that the sharing economy, in its spiritual essence, means oneness and identification with all that is through Self-realisation.

Let us be clear that none of these future transformations are foreseeable without the large-scale release of compassion and awareness throughout the human population, which must be nurtured and inspired by a new education based on more spiritual values. However ardently we embrace the idea of implementing a sharing economy in its most universal expression for the coming age, we are left with the reality of a modern era that is characterised by the greed and indifference of countless millions of individuals, and the systemic injustice of a corrupt world order that can hardly be ignored in any vision of a sustainable future.

This presents us with a challenge that requires much more than today's conventional education taught in a formal sense through schools and universities. There is also an urgent need of education in terms of becoming more spiritually aware of ourselves, an awareness that must somehow encompass our own divisive thinking that impedes the engagement of our hearts, and our unobserved social conditioning that serves to reproduce the separative ways of the past. The prevailing notion of a sharing economy is a notable case in point, for is it not all about ourselves and our self-regarding attitudes, as if humanity *in its entirety* is not a part of our everyday thinking and philosophies?

The lack of right education in every society therefore highlights our underlying dilemma, in that the sharing economy is a viable idea, a potentially colossal and planetary idea, but only if it is accomplished in an inclusive and moral way by concentrating our attention on the needs of the world's struggling poor majority. As we have forcefully argued, that is the only way a sharing economy can be properly sustained and steadily bourgeon over time. But have any of us been educated to share with those less fortunate than ourselves, even in the wealthiest democratic societies of North America, Western Europe and Australasia? Perhaps we need only bear witness to the global refugee crisis to see how far our education has strayed from a simple understanding of right human relations. For surely, if everyone was imbued with the values of sharing and cooperation from cradle to grave, then the crisis of mass human displacement that is caused by senseless regional conflicts—and largely contributed to by Western foreign policies—would never have reached this critical stage. But since it has manifested as a stark illustration of our unequal world, there can be no resolution to its deep-seated causes without the implementation of the principle of sharing into world affairs, thus returning us once again to our central premise.

We have so much yet to discover about the need for a more holistic or spiritual education to sustain a sharing economy, that for our present purposes we can only give a brief overview of its eventual form and transformative implications. Without question, the new education must eventually be seen in the form of school lessons for young children, who can be taught the meaning of sharing in basic social, economic and political terms, and thus informed as to why this simple principle is so important to our future wellbeing and survival. But we have also stressed how the principle of sharing is spiritual in its nature, and therefore requires teachings of a higher calibre that can inculcate an awareness of the inner self in any child or adult. Thus the individual may be led to perceive for themselves (through both a conscious understanding and an intuitive recognition) that humanity is one interdependent entity, inherently equal and potentially divine in its myriad of personality expressions.

Therefore to study the inner meaning of a sharing economy is, in the end, to arrive at an understanding of what many religious and spiritual thinkers refer to as the Art of Living. Unfortunately, a clear explanation of this term is difficult to convey at our current stage of human and spiritual evolution, when we are apparently so far away from the kind of education and social circumstances that will permit an understanding of life as a form of art. We also need to bear in mind that a deeper comprehension of this subject cannot be achieved without adequate knowledge of the spiritual constitution of man, for which the reader will need to refer to relevant books that provide more detailed information about the new educational methods and goals of the future, such as the writings of Alice A. Bailey.[27]

At the same time, much can be discovered for ourselves independently, through self-contemplation and logical reasoning, about how a new economic system based on the principle of sharing needs to go hand-in-hand with formidable changes in the inner awareness of mankind. To go further in this enquiry, it is beneficial to think of the social and cultural expression of a sharing economy in terms of the Art of Being, which is directly related to the Art of Living but far different in its meaning and implications. You cannot have one without the other, for the Art of Being relates to the inner side of life which is expressed outwardly in the world through our human relationships and varying modes of social organisation. We might simplify by saying that the Art of Being concerns the inner, whereas the Art of Living concerns the outer. Indeed, it is a spiritual platitude to say that man has to change from within if the world is to change, which is what the Art of Being principally refers to—namely, the unfoldment of the inherent divinity that exists within every individual and seeks expression through right human relations.

It is, therefore, the Art of Being that should most engross our attention at this time, and not the Art of Living as oft described, for it is the former that will largely define the new age education in its successive phases of evolvement. What that higher level of spiritual education may look like is beyond the scope of our present enquiry, although we can summarise by saying that it concerns an awareness of the soul and its purpose through meditation, spiritual disciplines, and service activity that is oriented to the general upliftment of mankind. Such are the eternal means by which we are progressively led towards Self-realisation (or the Art of Being), as attested to in the Ageless Wisdom teachings that have been released to humanity in diverse traditions throughout the millennia.[28] But even here we must acknowledge our difficulty of explanation, because you cannot practise or realise the Art of Being through a conditioned mind, or try to understand its meaning only intellectually. In fact, it is the very process of seeking the meaning of the Art of Being that will lead us to be gradually deconditioned, and therefore more consciously aware and inwardly free.

The previous statement alone may give us much to deliberate and cognise, simple though it may sound. For as long as we lack even an inchoate understanding of what the Art of Being means and represents along these lines, it is impossible to express the Art of Living on either an individual or group basis. This has always been the case within our inequitable societies that are failing to provide enough education and 'inner space' for the average person to apprehend, explore and demonstrate their soul's purpose.[29]

At most, we can merely engage in those social practices and altruistic behaviours that are the palest reflection of the Art of Living in our frenetic, distracted lives of today. Consider, for example, environmental recycling activities, charitable endeavours, and indeed the less commercialised aspects of the sharing economy in its localised forms. As worthwhile and often vital as these activities may be, they in no way represent a prevailing social awareness of what it means to live in harmlessness, simplicity and right relationship with respect to nature and all sentient beings. By definition, there is no 'art' to living unless we go inwards to investigate the reality of the inner self, and seek to manifest that awareness in our day-to-day life expression. The danger, otherwise, is that our activities will be based on imitation through wrong identification, for it is very easy to fake the appearance of a spiritual or ethical way of living that is nothing more than the fashionable following of others.

Notwithstanding our difficulties of verbal elucidation that compromise this discussion, it is still helpful to reflect upon the Art of Living as we enquire into the spiritual or inner meaning of a sharing economy. For this purpose, the Art of Living can be broadly defined as the growing awareness of right relationship and its individual and societal expression, including in our relationship to all the lower kingdoms of nature. But in any such definition again lies our problem, for how can we talk with clarity about a new way of living on this earth based on the correct orientation of man towards himself, his society and his natural environment, when we have yet to share the world's resources in a remotely equitable fashion?

It may take many generations before the common practice of the Art of Living—as distinguished by cooperation, consensus and trust, with all its associated inner qualities of honesty, sincerity, goodwill, humility, detachment and harmlessness—is the hallmark of our societies. Moreover, there can be no Art of Living that is sustained without the flourishing of compassion throughout the world, for such is the precondition for humanity to become more aware of the actual need for the Art of Being to guide our planetary evolution. In short, we are incapable of talking with precision or persuasive meaning on this subject, since it is the emerging civilisation that will exhibit the prevalent awareness of the Art of Being or Self-realisation, and thus be defined in its outer modes of social organisation.

PART IV

The esoteric significance
of the United Nations

Do we dare to dream, one day, of a United Nations that upholds a new civilisation based on a sharing economy, thus expressing right human relationship for the first time in millennia—and thus guiding each nation to realise its unique spiritual destiny?

In further contemplating this problem of awareness in sustaining a sharing economy, we may also discover the spiritual or esoteric significance of the United Nations, and the palpable connection that exists between the future advancement of this great international organisation and the corresponding advancement of a new education. If we rightly speak of a global sharing economy as being in its infancy today, then the United Nations is also in its earliest stage of demonstrating its highest economic, political and spiritual potential. But how will the United Nations achieve such an exalted role, where it becomes much more meaningful for humanity than just an intergovernmental institution with its assortment of bureaucratic offices and specialised agencies?

We must further engage with our intuition to answer this question, assuming we accept that the United Nations must one day express the fact of right relationship among its member states with their differing cultures and varying levels of material development. For indeed, right human relationship is clearly associated with the interaction of diverse groups of people, which we generally understand in terms of sovereign nations, distinct cultures and races. And it is the very presence and energy of a strengthened Assembly of Nations that can indirectly educate all those groups to raise their consciousness beyond a national, cultural or racial identity, thereby recognising our subjective inter-relationship and supra-identity as the one Humanity.

Unfortunately, most of us remain unaware of the future spiritual significance of the United Nations, and hence these observations are liable to sound like an indulgent flight of the imagination. For the time being, there are few who hold the United Nations in high esteem due to its many shortcomings and compromises. But we should be wary of dismissing its relevance out of hand before we have tried to grasp what its existence represents from the inner side of life. Let us try to visualise a day when the United Nations has its own specialised agency that is dedicated to the pooled, equitable sharing of surplus economic resources among the international community. This is the consummate vision of a sharing economy that symbolises world goodwill and the meaning of love in its broadest sense—which is to serve humanity in group formation. The United Nations can therefore enable those diverse groups that we term nations to demonstrate their soul purpose and, over time, begin to fulfil their spiritual destiny. This leads us to a profoundly expanded interpretation of a sharing economy, which not only concerns the right navigation of essential resources to prevent the ongoing tragedy of widespread human deprivation. Moreover, it signifies the beginning phase of nations becoming aware of themselves as evolving souls, yet without losing the unique attributes of their particular customs, traditions and cultures.

Does this help us to tentatively grasp how the United Nations may hasten the spiritual education of humanity through the principle of sharing? Again, we speak of education not specifically in the formal sense of schools and universities, but as the changes that will be brought about in human consciousness as a result of the United Nations' destined role in demonstrating the oneness of humanity. As much as the soul of each individual and nation has a spiritual purpose which is to serve humanity in line with the evolutionary Plan, it may be said that the United Nations has a hidden spiritual purpose which is to affirm and express the reality of the Kingdom of Souls as a visible fact on earth.

Let us put it this way: an unsurpassed mobilisation of all nations to end poverty and avert ecological disaster will represent the hearts of humanity putting the meaning of a sharing economy in its right place. At the same time, it will also represent the first stage of putting the United Nations in its right place through the dynamic manifestation of world goodwill. And that initial worldwide outpouring of goodwill may guide humanity to realise the greater meaning of soul purpose and right relationship which, as we have intimated, is to advance the Divine Plan in conscious cooperation with the Spiritual Hierarchy of our planet as it externalises outwardly on the physical plane.[30]

So there are several ways in which the United Nations can uphold the universal expression of right human relations and, by this means, serve to educate humanity:

> » By overseeing the implementation of the principle of sharing in world affairs, bringing about justice and balance in the distribution of resources between nations.
>
> » By providing a global organisational structure that can enable the Spiritual Hierarchy to carry out

the Divine Plan in conscious cooperation with humanity for the first time in untold millennia, and hence with unparalleled speed in our planetary evolution.

» By affirming the reality of the Kingdom of Souls on earth. This can be understood symbolically in the sense that Christ expresses the heart centre (love aspect) of humanity, while the United Nations may someday express the head centre (intelligence aspect) of humanity through its vastly expanded future activity in every department.[31]

For all these reasons, however far-fetched or abstruse they may seem at the present time, it is hopefully clear that any genuine conception of a sharing economy should be directed towards the relationship of the United Nations vis-à-vis the rest of the world, with an open mind towards its higher spiritual possibilities as an international law-making forum.

A simple metaphor that may spur our intuition is to think of the energy of Love being fragmented across this earth, almost like an immense jigsaw puzzle of planetary proportions. Hence it is up to every nation to solve this immense puzzle that is as old as humanity itself, for all the nations of the world represent an equally vital and unique piece. The means of putting those pieces back together again are verily simple, involving as it must the cooperative pooling of all the available finances, capacity and surplus resources of the family of nations, in order to address the culminating crises that threaten our continued evolution as a race. As the wealthiest countries begin to systematically share their resources with the less developed countries and vice versa, and as the idea of an emergency redistribution programme begins to be supported by ordinary people in massive and continual demonstrations, then the puzzle that we call Love will be gradually reassembled, step by step and piece by piece. Viewed in this way, perhaps we can envisage the importance of the United Nations to this historic transitional period we are currently undergoing—which will always be remembered as the time when humanity first applied the divine principle of sharing to our most urgent global priorities.

Upon returning our attention to the current world situation, we may question why we are reflecting on the meaning of a new spiritual education before humanity has experienced anything close to real peace or justice throughout the world. For what kind of all-inclusive education is it possible to achieve about the nature of the one Life that permeates the phenomenal universe, on a planet that allows millions of people to die in squalor without sufficient help from governments or the public at large? We may well accept, in a theoretical sense, that the implementation of the principle of sharing in world affairs is directly connected to the need for a governing United Nations Assembly and, eventually, to the equally vital need for new educational methods that can enable the Art of Living to unfold. But where do these speculative musings lead us today, if that education doesn't begin with every privileged person attending to the needs of the vulnerable, the weak and the dispossessed?

Always we must return to this central understanding, for if we want to rebuild our house then we must begin from its foundations. And the foundation of our misery in the 21st century is the fact that the shameful reality of avoidable human deprivation is still permitted to endure. To be spiritually educated also means to think clearly for oneself from the heart; so how else can we educate ourselves through the awareness of love at this time, if not to take action to prevent the neglect and exploitation of the poor, and finally end this age-old injustice?

PART V

The problem of modern technology

*Did you know that God is an amazing scientist
and a great artist whose creativity is not
yet understood, or even perceived?*

*What we call God is a spiritual idea, but without the
reality behind that idea you would not be reading
this—for God is nothing, and yet His breath
sustains the continuation of everything that is.*

*Was it not from a single spark of electricity
that your being and becoming was born?*

There are remaining questions that may occur to some readers concerning the potential of new technologies in changing the world, for the rapid growth of the internet and open source movements could be seen as a sign of humanity's readiness to share. But let us ask ourselves once more: are our modern technological innovations the true reflection of sharing as a divine principle, if they are not also directed towards improving the lives of everyone who lacks the essentials needed for a dignified and healthy life?

We are not suggesting there is anything wrong with the creative impetus towards innovation and progress, but the question is whether we can work on our cutting-edge projects in conjunction with an awareness of love. For love, in its simplest and unsentimental understanding, is summarised by the question: 'What about the others?'[32] Seemingly everyone today is preoccupied with the new digital discoveries and commercialised gadgets, especially the younger generations. But we are far from preoccupied with the injustice of poverty that is definitely worsening in most countries, no matter what is reported in the constantly revised and approximated global statistics.[33]

Rest assured that humanity will always be fascinated by its scientific and technological breakthroughs, which will continue whether or not there is rampant injustice throughout the world. Scientific investigation and creative innovation is a natural extension of man's inherent predisposition to explore his own constitution and the environing conditions of the earth, and gladly shall it ever remain. A more revelatory line of enquiry therefore involves the question of how technology will change its overall form and direction once the principle of sharing is in the process of controlling economic affairs, in accordance with our preceding discussion. What will happen if a significant number of humanity embrace the awareness that we are all one in creation, inherently equal and interdependent as a fact of nature, which means we cannot remain psychologically separated as a race any longer?

Surely the debates about whether certain technologies are beneficial or damaging for society will gradually dissolve over time, to be replaced with a prevailing concern for the right sharing of all technology in relation to mankind's social, economic and spiritual development. The present dilemmas about technology are only relevant to a world in which the hearts of humanity are generally suppressed through complacency, ignorance or indifference, while material desires are dominating the cultural norms and attitudes of the day. It could be said that superficial wants and needs are going through a social revolution throughout our consumer-driven world. Hence it is a manifestly unsustainable and insanely self-destructive world in which a spiritual revolution of the heart is yet to be witnessed, or even conceived of by most people.

Therefore some people enthusiastically welcome the increasing digitalisation of our economies and the relentless manufacture of high-tech goods that purportedly improve the quality of our lives—assuming, that is, we have the disposable income to afford them. Meanwhile, others decry the pernicious side-effects of those technologies that entrench the commercialisation of everyday life, and often go hand-in-hand with the erosion of civil liberties and basic human rights. But if the hearts of millions of people were awakened to the critical needs of others, and if the purpose of new technology was reconceived within a world that provides for the basic material and educational needs of everyone, would such a polarised debate last for very long?

The unfortunate victims of present trends are the world's children and unwary youth. They are an easy target for commercialised forms of technology that limit an individual's consciousness to an obsession with the material form, thereby impeding the growth of self-awareness. Of course, the problem lies not with the existence of modern technology as a medium for social progress, which overall has improved the living standards of the average family in economically advanced nations to a degree that would have been unimaginable before the industrial revolution. The problem, as ever, lies with the consciousness of man who accepts the benefits of those advances for a minority of the world population, sparing little thought for the millions of others whose lives remain untouched by any social improvements through whatever technological means.

Let us therefore ponder the significance of technology if it is truly used for the common good of all, instead of being co-opted by private interests and steered in an increasingly commercial direction. This may require a considerable leap of the imagination, considering how the problem originates with the hidden motives of any individual who discovers a new technological breakthrough, and then identifies with the object of their creation. As a result, the lower self or 'me' typically overshadows the process of innovation, which causes a new technology to be exploited for personal or material gain instead of being freely shared for the benefit of all. By extension, the multinational corporation with its concern for profit maximisation ultimately prevents any possibility of sharing the world's technology for the uplift and betterment of the entire race.

The ability to innovate may have come to humanity as a natural outgrowth of our urge to understand and consciously evolve, but it is an instinctive aptitude that was never meant to be monopolised by only the few, or else used as a tool for domination and control. Thus one has to ask: what is the relationship that exists between the evolution of technology and compassion? For if the right forms of technology were shared with the neediest people across the world, surely it would help so much to restore the health and wellbeing of countless suffering families. Let's not forget that medicines for AIDS and the many diseases of poverty are part of what we call technology too. Yet the pharmaceutical industries that develop these patented drugs are obviously not driven by a spirit of sharing and the common good, despite their wealth being based on the herbs and plants that are given freely by the earth for everyone to use. So if one begins to look at these issues with a compassionate attitude to life, we are led to ask why every medicine and healthcare advance has not been given freely to humanity as a whole—with implications that go to the heart of all that is wrong with our ailing civilisation.[34]

These are some of the most preliminary considerations before we can even begin to grasp the future role of technology in a world that has long established a viable sharing economy, thus enabling all people to enjoy the same equal rights, opportunities and fundamental freedoms. At such a time and not before, we may begin to foresee the higher purposes of technology that advance in synchronicity with the spiritual evolution of mankind. We are currently witnessing the merest intimations of these future possibilities with the rise of robots and automation, leading to much anxiety about the prospect of pervasive unemployment and spiralling inequalities when the fruits of machine-produced wealth are not equitably shared. Hence the difficulty in contemplating a more egalitarian and peaceful world where super-machines serve to liberate mankind to contemplate and study the reality of the inner self, and ultimately give every individual the space and freedom to pursue the Art of Being or Self-realisation.

Here we must return to our discussion on the necessity of introducing a new type of education, which will progressively call for the establishment of spiritually-oriented schools that are geared towards studying the Ageless Wisdom teachings and the Science of the Soul. Much more has been written on this subject in the aforementioned writings of Alice A. Bailey and others, and it lies outside the scope of our current remit, except to note a further link between the new education and future technologies that is rooted in the awakening of man's spiritual nature. The fact is that as new forces and spiritual energies flood the world, technology has a great role to play in speeding up the evolution of human consciousness. Yet most contemporary writers on this subject remain unaware of the deeper spiritual meaning and import of technological progress. Indeed, its future potential can never be comprehended, in all simplicity, through a concrete analysis of the transitory material forms.

The esoteric significance of technology is denoted by the phrase 'mind over matter', which concerns the ability of man to control his environment and unlock the hidden potentialities of nature by working in harmony with presently unseen and scientifically unknown evolutionary forces. Our partial unravelling of the mystery of electricity, for example, is a small indication of the undreamt of powers inherent in the universe that man can someday utilise. But this will only become apparent when mankind's attitudes are oriented towards the service of the race, and our predominant motives are defined by an inclusiveness that is unhindered by commercial, nationalistic or self-seeking objectives. The reader may already know that the invention of the telephone symbolises man's innate ability to telepathise. Correspondingly, the invention of the internet symbolises the awareness of the One World or omniscient consciousness that is the due inheritance of the Self-realised Adept.[35] Our future technological developments will accelerate beyond all measure when man discovers his latent capacity to control the outer life of form through the inner faculties of his directed mind. Some day, it may even result in the scientific discovery of the existence of the soul. And when the evolution of technology finally moves in line with an awareness of the Divine Plan for humanity's spiritual evolution, we may also witness how technology provides the complex logistical solutions required for an advanced system of bartering and exchange to be facilitated worldwide, as per our earlier reflections.

In sum, these remarks are merely intended to help us grasp how our conceptualisations are severely limited by our present lack of understanding of divine purpose and the higher cosmological laws which condition all phenomena. To be sure, the expansion of technology is forever intertwined with the expansion of human consciousness—and neither can proceed on its correct path until the entrenched social, political, economic, psychological and spiritual divisions of the modern world are on course to being reversed.

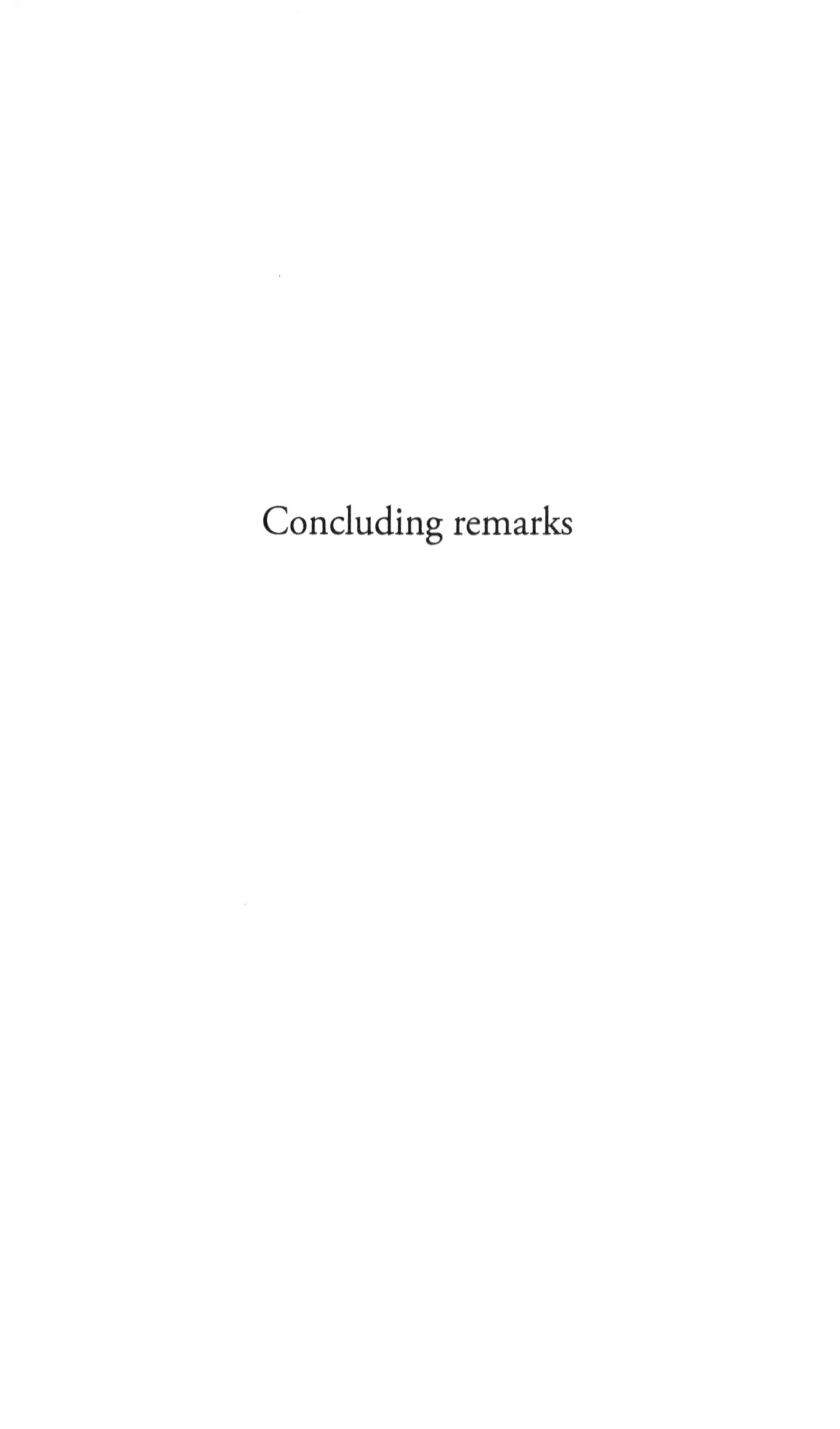

Concluding remarks

Whether or not we are able to tune with these introductory reflections about the inner and holistic meaning of a sharing economy, it is hoped that the reader is at least convinced of the paramount importance of implementing the principle of sharing into world affairs. The more that technology is shared, for example, the more our understanding can grow of what technology can achieve as a beneficent tool for mankind's spiritual evolution. And the more that humanity calls for the sharing of global resources to end the economic insecurity and exploitation of the majority poor, the more our awareness will grow of what the sharing economy means in its farthest reaching modes and means of expression.

Let us reiterate our most important observation for those who promote a sharing economy in its presently limited forms. Hopefully it is clear that we are putting the cart before the horse if we believe that a community vision of sharing is a lasting solution to humanity's problems. Are we yet convinced that the localised methods of sharing will only burgeon and become all-inclusive, once a sharing economy is at the definite stage of being implemented as a global multilateral process?[36]

When the richest nations are genuinely sharing their wealth and resources with the least developed world regions, and when the wider public is directing the idea of economic sharing from the heart to where it most belongs—that is when the practice of sharing on a community-led basis will blossom beyond our wildest dreams. For then the whole world will be involved, including the several billion people whose basic rights to life and liberty were unfulfilled beforehand. And then the energy that we call love will be awakened and released among a vast swathe of everyday citizens, leading to inner and outer transformations that we have never witnessed before in our societies—an outpouring of joy and goodwill, a perceivable lessening of stress and tension worldwide, a newfound sense of trust and hope among the rich and poor alike…

Put simply, the climaxing world situation is impelling us to place the needs of the world and the poor first, not our pockets or our self-centred interests. Otherwise, our idea of sharing on a community level will inevitably flounder in the wake of mounting trends towards an ever more divided, commercialised and indifferent world. We will be like the politician who promises a better society to a largely passive electorate. Those promises may seem real and honest at the time, until they evaporate within a newly elected government that is bound by the dictates of its corporate benefactors. In the same way, what can come of a sharing economy vision that is confined in its expression to the relatively few affluent people in a wholly profit-oriented and materialistic culture? And when the only significant form of sharing that is enacted on a global and political level among allied governments—relative to the constraints of *realpolitik*—is the sharing of armaments, information and covert intelligence?

We have emphasised how the sharing economy concerns the navigation of energy and resources to its right place, from the physical essentials of food, finance and other basic material resources, to the intangible qualities of empathy and awareness that must be expanded to encompass the good of the whole. Furthermore, we have reasoned that the rampant and malefic forces of commercialisation work against this hoped-for eventuality, where the sharing economy idea is understood inclusively and holistically as the means to create balance and right human relations on this earth. Hence even the phrase 'a sharing economy' has been misunderstood and misplaced, and it has inevitably fallen into the wrong hands. Even many of those sharing proponents with the best intentions have failed to realise the devious power of the forces of commercialisation, which on this issue is like a cat who plays with a mouse it has caught, before slowly devouring it bit by bit.

A transformative vision of the sharing economy can go nowhere without the engaged heart to sustain it and the intelligent mind to structure its expression in society. In the absence of which, we see how quickly the idea of sharing can be degraded into profitmaking and business activity. But when the heart centre of humanity is visibly awakened, when we together call for a just redistribution of resources to save our needlessly dying brethren, then we will see how the true sharing economy vision will suddenly begin to speak for itself, and for the very first time.

Can you recall how happy people were the world over when President Obama was initially elected to office, at least in those early days of expectation that American foreign policies would be redirected from the pursuit of imperial hegemony?[37] Then be assured that the day governments commit to sharing the world's resources will bring about a joy amongst humanity that will be many, many times more powerful and real. For there is another tsunami that we have yet to experience in its fullest measure, one that is beneficent and not malefic as a physical force—and that is a tsunami of love. A force so great that when it hits you, it will bring you to your knees. A force that will lift you up in your varied endeavours with a new kind of energy, a new kind of clarity, a new kind of creativity and strength. It is a force that all the sharing economy advocates should look towards and embrace, for it will be backed by millions upon millions of other adherents within every country, from the wealthiest suburbs to the poorest shantytowns that contain a wellspring of hope for transforming our world.

*

Perhaps the serious reader still seeks some pragmatic words of advice in these closing remarks, for whose purpose the following sentiments are offered. The present author acknowledges the immense difficulty in creating a worldwide movement for a sharing economy, as long as the word 'sharing' has not entered the vocabulary or imaginations of the bulk of political activists. So for the time being, we must do what we can by joining the existing movements for freedom and justice in their various expressions, many of which stem from the problem of unequal wealth and resource distribution as we have acknowledged.

At the same time, we should also dig deeper into our understanding of sharing and cooperation in its holistic expression, and contemplate the transformative potential of these universal principles when applied to the interconnecting crises facing humanity. Let not the political idea of sharing remain an intellectual concept, when the world needs this principle to be implemented as an economic process between nations if humanity is to survive, for the growing gap between the haves and have-nots contains within it the seeds of our own destruction. Thus it is critical that the sharing economy idea is expanded globally in our thinking and endeavours, most especially towards the least privileged members of the human family—as per the oft-repeated premise of our enquiry.

We may repeat until we are hoarse that the true meaning of a sharing economy is only to be found in relation to the world's impoverished majority, but unless that awareness is translated into lively discussions and actions that are focused on ending extreme deprivation within an immediate timeframe, it means very little at all. There is nothing to stop us from getting engaged in those ongoing activities, or to form groups of sharing economy advocates that are concerned with expanding this creative concept into a new frontier. We have already spelled out what must be done, which is to press our governments to share their surplus resources through the United Nations and its relevant agencies, in order to finally bring about that long-declared aspiration to achieve freedom from want for all peoples everywhere.

So by all means, let's carry on with our community-oriented activities that embody the principle of sharing in some measure. But can we not also reverse the direction of those activities at least once a week, and urge our political representatives to employ a sharing economy for the hungry and destitute poor, both at home and far abroad? Just consider the number of people who are already engaged with the various sharing economy ideas and initiatives, as generally understood and applied within the predominantly affluent parts of Western society. What is to stop those well-meaning groups from uniting with a single demand on a weekly basis, and petitioning their governments to redistribute the nation's surplus produce towards this honourable and uplifting cause of ending poverty?

The longer we fail to pursue such a simple course of action, the more our idea of sharing will reveal itself to have no soul, no purpose, and no future with any meaning. What purpose is it all for, anyway, if we only attach our ideas of prosperity and sharing to our own particular community, culture or nation? In a world that is increasingly divided in two between those who have more than enough and those who have nothing at all, our ideas will eventually become inhuman and destined to collapse, unless we think about the needs of others too!

It may be misconstrued that saving the poor and starving masses is the only reason for promoting our vision of a sharing economy, which is actually far from the case. What we are most concerned with is the need to bring awareness, love and common sense to our everyday thinking and actions. It only happens that our prevalent lack of thinking about the welfare of others is what most overtly demonstrates the absence of these long-suppressed human attributes. We need to ask ourselves why we are interested in saving those who are needlessly dying from poverty-related causes, if we don't consider them equal to ourselves with a divine right to spiritually evolve. Is that not the reason, above all reasons, why we can no longer allow any person to die as a result of our collective indifference, when there is more than enough food and other resources available for everyone in the world?

By the same token, it is erroneous to believe that the United Nations is ultimately the greatest hope we have for healing, repairing and renewing the world, when the only real hope lies in awakening the spiritual heart centre of humanity as a whole. Is there any other factor that can bring about the phenomenal transformations we need, if not the compassion and awareness that leads to the correct motivations for navigating energy and resources to the right place? Please meditate and carefully reflect upon this last rhetorical question, as it may reveal much about how we can personally be of use to the great work of planetary renewal that lies ahead.

ANNEX

The gift economy and barter

There is a great deal that could be said about our understanding of the gift economy in relation to barter and sharing the world's resources (see chapter two). In basic economic terms, barter is simply understood as the direct exchange of goods or services without the use of money. In contrast, the social practise of gifting entails no expectation of immediate reciprocation or any explicit agreement of future reward, monetary or otherwise. Both practices of gifting and bartering are thought to have preceded the invention of money as a medium of exchange.

However, conventional economic thinking posits that barter was the most prevalent mode of exchange in ancient civilisations (presumably from the Neolithic period), and the inefficiency of barter was a driving force in the creation of monetary systems. Introductory economics textbooks still espouse the essential ideas of Adam Smith in *The Wealth of Nations*, in which the primitive nature of bartering among individuals—leading to a 'coincidence of wants'—prevented the specialisations needed for the expansion of trade and markets. The propensity to 'truck, barter and exchange one thing for another', in Smith's famous words, is viewed as a product of man's inherent predisposition to maximise his own inherent, competitive self-interest.

Anthropologists have long established that there is a lack of historical evidence to support these views. No example of a pure barter economy exists; on the contrary, ethnographic data suggests that gift-giving was the most usual means of exchanging goods and services in archaic societies, often tied to elaborate customs and kin networks. As Marcel Mauss argued in his classic monologue, *An Essay on the Gift*, the core feature of pre-market social systems was not a calculative kind of profiteering at each other's expense, but rather the fostering of intimate communal ties based on reciprocity and redistribution. Generosity and sharing, not selfishness, was the everyday norm. These anthropological findings have offered profound insights into the nature of trust and solidarity, and also challenge some of the founding ideas of the modern discipline of economics—particularly the simplistic neoclassical conception of *homo-economicus*.

Many thinkers are concerned with how to apply the nature of gift economies to our modern consumerist world. Returning 'the spirit of the gift' to all aspects of human life clearly has immense implications for contemporary societies where the opposite values are encouraged—that is, hoarding over sharing and free circulation; competition and greed over altruistic cooperation. Much has been written about the problems of our debt-based monetary system that serves to concentrate wealth upwards, that inhibits our innate desire to freely give and express gratitude, and that depletes the commons of nature and society through ownership, profit and interest. It is very hopeful to see activists who are motivated to translate gift ideology into a new gift politics, thus perceiving the need to shrink the monetary realm in everyday life and rejuvenate human relationships outside of the sphere of quantifiable economics.

What's interesting from our perspective is how barter is still viewed in a negative light by conservative and radical thinkers alike. David Graeber, for example, in his illustrious book *Debt: The First 5,000 Years*, argues that the only evidence of barter occurring in pre-modern times was between strangers or even enemies, where 'the mantle of sociability is extremely thin' and 'no sense of mutual responsibility or trust' exists. Thus a society based on barter could only 'be one in which everybody was an inch from everybody else's throat'. Marshall Sahlins, author of *Stone Age Economics*, adopts similar arguments and identifies a scheme of reciprocity between gifting and bartering, with the latter being the most negative where each party intends to profit from the exchange, often at the expense of the other.

Karl Polyani, in his landmark work *The Great Transformation*, also argues at length against the fallacy of man's propensity to barter as the foundation of earlier civilisations. He appears to view barter, or 'higgling and haggling', in much the same vein as profit-oriented commercial exchange, and as the opposite of reciprocity and redistribution where the logic of the economy is embedded in social relations. Karl Marx in *Capital I* and *Grundisse* says nothing to contradict these basic assumptions, in which barter is seen as motivated by the mutual advantages it affords to both parties, if not directly by profit-seeking then indirectly by personal gain. Still today, barter is typically viewed as an impersonal transaction that people only partake in for petty, infrequent or emergency transactions, such as in the wake of the collapse of national economies.

The question, therefore, is whether we can expand our understanding of barter beyond this trivial notion of 'swapping things in such a way as to seek mutual advantage'? This book reasons that our common perception of a sharing economy is extremely limited in its current ideations and expressions (as usually conceived of in solely personal or localised terms), and much the same can be said of barter. Of course, there has always been a dark and unfair side to bartering throughout human history, up until our day—such as the antiquated cultural practice of paying for brides with camels. But are we able to perceive, however dimly in these times, how barter and the gift economy are potentially one and the same, and aligned upon the same evolutionary trajectory?

Here we are pointing to the contours of a new civilisation which surprisingly few academic thinkers contemplate, whereby barter economies are instituted at a far higher level of organisation and motivated by the joy of sharing and loving attention (the antidote to profit). I submit that there is an entire philosophy of barter yet to be discovered, and a way of life that many tribal cultures of the past have exemplified to some degree, and which must now be resurrected and reapplied to our interdependent world economies.

Still it remains to be seen how we can awaken the ancient spirit of the gift in a world that is submerged in extreme inequality, injustice and pain, and that has lived outside of the gift mentality for millennia. My own position on the subject should be clear from the chapters above, for the poorest regions of the global South are crying out for a gift economy that is instituted multilaterally among nation states. It may be construed that the Brandt Report was essentially aiming in this direction with its 'programme of priorities' and call for a large-scale transfer of resources to developing countries, especially the poverty belts of Africa and Asia. I may have interpreted

Brandt's proposal as an incipient attempt to create a global sharing economy, but for the famished poor who receive such emergency resource transfers it is surely perceived, consciously or not, as a gift from God. Thus the gift economy, the sharing economy—both are intrinsically interrelated.

That said, it isn't a practical strategy to mobilise a grassroots citizens' movement around the concept of the gift, or to approach leading politicians in such a vein. We have to demand: 'Let's share the world's resources!' So I do not believe in the revolutionary potential of the gift, for it will never produce, in and of itself, an uprising of the masses towards right human relationship. I believe only in the power of the people united. That is why all of my enquires return to the same vision of heralding Article 25 with millions of other individuals and groups worldwide, which will represent a U-turn in human consciousness. It is not about rendering the economy 'sacred', as some have suggested, but rather of realising en masse that Article 25 of the Universal Declaration holds within itself the sacredness of humanity, or shall we say the realisation of humanity's oneness. And if the gift economy advocate doesn't mention the emergency of the dying poor and hungry, then the same arguments apply as to the sharing economy enthusiasts (see chapter one)—for then it is all about ourselves and our like-minded adherents once again, without an awareness defined by the attitude: 'What about the others?'

What is most important to emphasise is the new vision that will arise as a result of sharing the world's resources, a vision that expands far beyond our present ideas and conceptualisations of social betterment. Non-monetary modes of fair and equitable economic exchange will inevitably proliferate, for the systematised sharing of essential resources between and within nations will naturally create new laws, new rules and new institutions on state and inter-state levels. Debt as we know it today—whether for sovereign states, governments, companies or individuals—will gradually lose its hold and relevance in economic affairs.

No doubt this vision may require us to project our consciousness many centuries hence, and there is no predicting how it will unfold. Perhaps only catastrophe shall spur the development of barter economies on a local to a global scale, as we have also hinted in the concluding remarks of this book. One way or another, our usage of money as a medium of exchange will have to evolve and assume a more beneficent mode of expression, until it gradually ceases to dominate human relations. To be sure, money is not the root of all evil, as said the Apostle Paul, but man's selfish motivation for profit assuredly is. How great, then, are the laws that stem from the implementation of the principle of sharing, just one branch of which concerns the development of barter macroeconomics for a future non-profit-based world.

Thus it is possible to intuitively foresee the evolutionary trend of world events towards a global pooling of surplus resources, where each nation 'barters' with other nations through a multilateral exchange mechanism. All shall be aware of the common needs, produce and capacities of all, and all may come and freely take what they lack from the global pool. An expanded definition of barter therefore concerns the navigation of energy and resources to the right place, and in the right measure. The meaning of 'exchange', in this enlarged context, does not necessarily imply an immediate reciprocation based on exact equivalence, for it is reasonable to imagine a universal credit system that determines the value of bartered goods that are received and redistributed. Let us be in no doubt that such a system would have to be colossal in magnitude, and highly technologically sophisticated in its scientific exactitude. The existence of food banks today may provide a miniature clue of a different organising principle of economic organisation, provided we can extrapolate that example to a world order in which the very idea of charity is a long forgotten remnant of humanity's past.

If this sounds like a utopian dream, then let us observe the evolution of bartering that is already happening in our societies. Electronic money, alone, is an augur of things to come as currency moves from the physical to the digital realm. There are also many forms of bartering that are not material but relational in nature, such as through the internet and social networking technologies, or in terms of the free exchange of our creative ideas and imaginations. Similar observations can be made about the gift economy, in the sense that it affects the individual to reciprocate (i.e. gratefully receive and desire to give back) in a voluntary manner, and on the basis of goodwill. When viewed in this light, the gift economy effectively engenders barter, and barter engenders the gift economy. Hence the imperative need to implement the principle of sharing in world affairs, which will enable the spirituality of bartering and gifting to naturally arise. So it is not simply a matter of sharing resources and meeting our needs without the use of money. Every social and economic transaction must also be informed and motivated by our felt divinity within, and with an educated understanding of the Ageless Wisdom.

Such is our repeated argument: that a just sharing of the earth's resources will never be accomplished unless it is animated by the Christ Principle, and is thus an expression of the joy of living. Perhaps this explains why the Brandt Report was never taken seriously in the 1980s, for there was no evidence of this 'inner' quality of love animating public policy decisions, either from the political class or the wider populace. One might say that an emergency redistribution programme should be motivated by the spirit of the gift and sharing, but it is really a matter of awareness born of necessity. Once we are aware of our brother's needs, those needs must necessarily become the measure of our actions. Thus we navigate the world's energy and resources to the right place, and in the right measure.

Remember that the spiritual and holistic meaning of the sharing economy is 'to be with' in all respects, as we explained at the beginning of chapter two. In the same way, the spirit of the gift can be described from this inner angle in terms of awareness, common sense, and loving understanding. Barter, in its higher spiritual correspondences, is also sustained by these same inner qualities, and consequently breeds trust, intelligence, creativity and wisdom. The esoteric counterpart of both the gift and barter economy is harmony, equilibrium and unity within diversity, although we have not yet reached a time when the higher meaning of these spiritual principles and laws are commonly apprehended by mankind.

Our observations here are encircling the beauty of the love of God, from which viewpoint barter can be understood as a part of planetary spiritual law and order. It is an expression of divine perception, in itself. It is the integral economic facilitator of humanity's future spiritual evolution, let us say. Therefore the gift economy, the barter economy, the sharing economy—all are born of the presence of divinity. And without the perennial existence of the divine principle of sharing, none of these ideas and social practices would ever have arisen (or rearisen in our modern times). We could also describe the gift economy as part of the commons of humanity, if it is perceived through the lens of compassion and spiritual awareness—but that is a diverging line of enquiry to be explored in a separate book.[38] All I am seeking to point out is how many thinkers and activists are trying to open the door to the principle of sharing, even if they deign to use the word 'sharing' and remain unconscious of their deepest inspiration from the soul level.

As far as I am concerned, the gift economy concept is another philosophical analysis of sharing, one that is curiously related to theorists of the commons and arguably more sophisticated than advocates for community-based sharing economies. So many transformative political theories are left sitting on the shelves and awaiting their time to come. The principle of sharing is the greatest law of human evolution that will explode in many thousands of different ideas, old and new. Then another time shall come, one hopes, when all this complicated phraseology will melt and be replaced by a much simpler understanding of life, in direct proportion to our experience of the joy of living. All these economic concepts are like intellectual ripples of the principle of sharing, or like brothers and sisters with different qualities who remain united by their same mother, which we term compassion. No philosophy of man has ever focused mainstream thought on the Lighted Way, or mutually led us to the right embrace of divinity. Yet it is all about love at the end of the day. So rather than talk about a gifting, a bartering or a sharing economy per se, why don't we talk about a love economy? That might be too simple for our presently complex humanity, but what is spiritually advanced is also, indeed, veritably simple.

Endnotes

1 It may be helpful for the reader to note a marked contradiction that remains between two competing visions of economic sharing, as alluded to throughout chapter one. On the one hand, there are those who reject the materialistic attitudes that have defined recent decades, and who perceive the need for an entirely different way of living that is characterised by connectedness and sharing, rather than ownership and conspicuous consumption. This is the tech-savvy generation of Millennials who embrace the ethic of 'sharing more and owning less', and to whom the first chapter of this book was principally addressed. On the other hand, many entrepreneurial individuals hold a very different idea of a sharing economy that involves new business start-ups whose raison d'être is revenue growth, shareholder value maximisation and the monopolisation of markets. Numerous commentators have questioned whether these commercialised internet platforms are in any way compatible with genuine sharing per se, and thus capable of bringing us closer to a more equitable, just and sustainable world.

From this writers perspective, it is a feat of Orwellian doublespeak to conflate the noble principle of sharing with for-profit business ventures that cater to a minority of affluent consumers, and mainly in high-income countries. Ongoing legal challenges over worker exploitation and low regulation have revealed the true nature and direction of this consumer-to-consumer (C2C) model of sharing resources. Not to mention the vast fortunes already made by the pioneers of such online social networks and electronic markets. Clearly, the essential dynamic of for-profit enterprise—to marketise formerly non-economic spheres of life—is no different in the internet-enabled sharing economy than in the dominant corporate sector. By monetising our skills, personal belongings and community activities, the line between the market and non-market worlds is increasingly blurred and intermeshed, which only serves to reinforce the profit imperatives of consumerist societies. While it is not our intention to provide a detailed critique or typology of the sharing economy in its present understanding, we would agree with many others that the commercial usage of this term is, at best, disingenuous and misleading. More appropriate terms in common usage include crowd-based capitalism, collaborative consumption, the platform economy, access economy, renting economy, or the on-demand economy, among others.

2   Contrary to the common misconception that people are individualistic and selfish by nature, anthropologists have shown that gifting and sharing has long formed the basis of community relationships in societies across the world. A recent spate of scientific research has built on this evidence to demonstrate that as human beings we are naturally predisposed to cooperate and share in order to maximise our chances of survival and collective wellbeing. Without the act of sharing and reciprocity, there would be no social foundations upon which to build societies and

economies. For a review of academic thought, see for example: Jeremy Rifkin, *The Empathic Civilization*, Cambridge: Polity Press, 2009; Michael Tomasello, *Why We Cooperate*, Cambridge: MIT Press, 2009; Frans De Waal, *The Age of Empathy*, New York: Harmony Books, 2009; Colin Tudge, *Why Genes are Not Selfish and People are Nice*, Floris books, 2013.

3   During the period between 2011 and 2016, our campaigning group Share The World's Resources (STWR) emphasised this simple perspective at many events that were focused on promoting the sharing economy concept. With few exceptions, the politics of sharing and its macroeconomic dimensions were neglected in these forums, which were generally concerned with solely interpersonal (peer-to-peer) and/or commercialised forms of collaboration. STWR therefore argued the necessity of broadening our understanding and interpretation of what constitutes a sharing economy. It stands to reason that long-term, systemic issues like climate change and social inequality must be tackled through government policies and effective national legislation. Indeed, the basic social functions of the state can be understood as a form of collective economic sharing. Through the process of progressive taxation and redistribution, for example, we share a portion of the nation's financial resources (personal income and assets, as well as company profits) for the benefit of society as a whole. Governments must redistribute a large proportion of tax revenue to ensure that the wider population can access essential goods and services such as healthcare, education, housing and utilities, as well as other important forms of social security. Universal systems of welfare and public service provision—however inefficiently administered—are clearly an expression of social justice that can reduce inequalities and strengthen social cohesion within countries. In such a light, the financial austerity measures imposed on a majority of countries

following the 'Great Recession' (2007-2009) can be considered the antithesis of a sharing economy by any sensible definition.

This may not be a particularly radical interpretation, but the fact remains that a vast majority of the world population lack comprehensive social protection guarantees—almost four out of every five people, according to the International Labour Organisation. Yet many low-income countries simply do not have the resources they need to build effective tax systems that can finance universal social protection and facilitate economic development. These realities point to the urgent need for scaling up new forms of economic sharing between countries as well as within them. Given the tremendous levels of wealth that exist alongside extreme poverty and destitution, it is imperative that we extend the principles that underpin national systems of sharing to encompass the entire family of nations. This has dramatic implications for, in particular, the current arrangements of overseas aid, which should at least be converted into an international system of pooled funding and automatic transfers, as proposed over many decades. Longstanding proposals also exist for a Global Fund for Social Protection that can help poorer States to meet the gap between what they are able to provide and a minimal social protection floor, in line with human rights commitments. What we are attempting to indicate here is a wider understanding of what the sharing economy means in political terms, of which there are, of course, many other aspects beyond the domain of social and economic policy. For further introductory perspectives, see: Share The World's Resources, 'Financing the Global Sharing Economy', October 2012, www.sharing.org/financing; 'A Primer on Global Economic Sharing', June 2014, www.sharing.org/primer; 'A Collection of Resources on the Sharing Economy', May 2014, www.sharing.org/sharing-economy

4   See note 6.

5   For more on this theme, see: Mohammed Sofiane Mesbahi, 'Commercialisation: The antithesis of sharing', in *Studies on the Principle of Sharing*, Matador books, 2020.

6   This poses an instructive line of enquiry for the interested reader, for whose purpose the following brief sketch is offered as a prompt for further reflection and study. We might begin by examining the historical roots of our unequal world system in the processes of plunder and extraction that defined the colonial era. Since at least the fifteenth century, incalculable riches were siphoned out of the global South to chiefly finance Europe's industrial revolution. Through conquest, enclosure, slavery and violent dispossession, a free market system was fashioned across the non-Western world for the benefit of wealthy elites in Western Europe and, later, the United States. Thus defined the first 'golden era' of globalisation, in which the core of the world economic system was designed to extract raw materials and wealth from its periphery, to exploit its labour and to provide new markets for the West's surplus goods. It is important that we study this painful history in order to understand the origins of the stark inequality between rich and poor nations.

    It wasn't until the post-war period that optimism began to grow among the formerly colonised nations of Africa, Asia and Latin America. Many Southern countries experimented with more autonomous models of national development, based on a strong interventionist role for governments and less reliance on the exports of cheap raw materials. On the global level, it was hoped that the United Nations could act as a conduit for a New International Economic Order to right the economic and social injustice of previous years. The UN Conference on Trade and Development (UNCTAD) was formed to articulate the needs of developing countries, with a view to restructuring the world order for the purpose of removing its inequalities and imbalances. But far from welcoming a fairer distribution of the world's resources, the dominant industrialised nations—newly christened as the Group of Seven—manoeuvred to further sideline the UN's role in global economic governance. As a Third World debt crisis mounted, the stage was set for the International Monetary Fund (IMF) and World Bank to step into the fray during the 1980s and push loans that were conditional on 'structural adjustment' policies. This marked a dramatic reversal in economic orthodoxy: stricken governments across the global South were forced to liberalise markets, reduce barriers to trade, privatise state-owned enterprises, conduct massive public sector layoffs, and even cut basic social services and subsidies on essential foodstuffs. Under the pressure to maintain obligations to creditors, social safety nets were often decimated and money diverted from public goods such as healthcare, education and aid to small-scale farmers.

The so-called neoliberal doctrine that underpinned these programmes represented, in effect, the abandonment of the redistributive agenda in promoting human development—a prospect that was anathema to the UN's founding vision and that would have been unthinkable in the 1950s or 1960s. It put an end to the former policies of national self-reliance and import substitution that aimed to help Southern countries regain some control over their domestic economies. Instead, the IMF and World Bank restructuring process—applied in over 70 countries—compelled recipient governments to dismantle state-led economic structures and expand the scope of the free market which inevitably benefited more competitive Northern interests. Many critics have argued that the real purpose was not to help poorer countries develop, but to roll back their gains of previous decades and get a tighter grip over their economic and financial destinies. Over the last 50 years, the nexus of power in the world economy has increasingly shifted towards major transnational corporations, multilateral banks, and trading regimes that are heavily biased in favour of rich country priorities.

An analysis of data from the UN and other institutions provides a damning indictment of this extreme market-driven model of globalisation. The development industry always promised a closing gap between rich and poor countries, yet inequality has continued to explode since the 1960s (whether measured in terms of per capita incomes or various financial resource flows). The picture is complex, as some emerging markets have benefited from increased inflows of foreign capital (like China, Hong Kong, South Korea, Taiwan and Malaysia), while other regions have never been profitably integrated into the world economy, especially across sub-Saharan Africa. Modern globalisation has led to widening income disparities within almost all nations, and created new super-divisions of winners and losers. Possibly two-thirds of humanity are exempted from the global chains of production and consumption that benefit the wealthiest citizens, which some have described as an increasing trend of global economic apartheid in the twenty-first century. It is impossible for us to summarise in this footnote the sweeping institutional reforms that are needed at the global level to reverse these trends, or the macroeconomic policies of sharing that should underpin a new vision of sustainable development. It may suffice here if we emphasise the persistent reality: that the poorest countries as a whole remain net exporters of capital and resources to the North, despite the growing impoverishment of their societies. That the lavish lifestyles of the affluent are effectively financed by the poverty of the majority world, while wholly inadequate measures of overseas aid and philanthropic activity mask the systemic injustices of the global economy.

7   The World Economic Forum (WEF) is an international foundation established in 1971 where political and business

leaders gather for its invitation-only annual meeting, held at the end of January each year in Davos, Switzerland. Campaigners for global justice have often mobilised during this time of year to expose the distorted worldview and hypocrisies of a privileged global elite. The World Social Forum, for example, was conceived as a counterpoint to the corporate vision of globalisation upheld at Davos; each social forum was held around the same time to promote alternative answers to world economic problems, as encapsulated by the slogan 'Another world is possible'. Discussions at Davos ostensibly focus on key issues of planetary concern, particularly the extreme discrepancies in living standards within and between countries. Notably, the 2015 meeting adopted the slogan 'sharing and caring'. But as campaigning groups like Oxfam have often illustrated, the only kind of sharing that is championed at Davos is within the context of charity or philanthropy, as opposed to real solutions that require government interventions and a more equitable sharing of wealth, power and resources. To be sure, Oxfam regularly use the WEF annual meetings to highlight gaping global inequalities, in which private billionaire wealth is increasingly soaring to record heights. The year after the WEF's founder, Klaus Schwab, espoused the slogan of 'sharing' in 2015, Oxfam famously revealed how the richest 1 percent of humanity own more wealth than the poorest half of the world combined.

8   In 2015, all 193 UN Member states ratified the 2030 Agenda for Sustainable Development which contained 17 interlinked goals. Known as the Sustainable Development Goals (SDGs) or 'Global Goals', these comprise a detailed list of targets and indicators with many laudable aims—above all, to 'end poverty in all its forms everywhere' and 'leave no-one behind'. Unlike their predecessors called the Millennium Development Goals, the SDGs apply to countries of both the global North and

South, while also including many ambitious environmental targets. However, civil society groups have roundly criticised the Goals for failing to challenge the deeper structural causes of our planetary crises. Nor do they explicitly reflect the necessity of redistributing resources more equally within and among nations. In the present context of global economic recession, a decline in development aid, the downsizing of UN operations and a retreat from multilateral cooperation, there is little prospect of the SDGs achieving their proclaimed transformational vision. For more background, see: Share The World's Resources, 'Beyond the Sustainable Development Goals: Uncovering the truth about global poverty', September 2015, www.sharing.org/sdgs

9   cf. Mohammed Sofiane Mesbahi, *Heralding Article 25: A People's Strategy for World Transformation*, Matador books, 2016 (see Part I: The failure of governments).

10   To justify the growing gulf between rich and poor worldwide, it has often been repeated by governments and multilateral agencies that extreme poverty levels have steadily decreased worldwide since the 1980s. The World Bank has consistently painted an upbeat picture of the global poverty situation, which usefully supports the prevailing ideological belief in free markets and liberalisation policies. As long as the poor are slowly becoming better off, the immense wealth of the few generated by corporate globalisation can be viewed as beneficial for everyone. But reputed analysts have long criticised the World Bank's statistics on many counts, particularly for its arbitrarily low income poverty line—once fixed at $1 per day and now modified to $1.90 per day. Adults and children living just above this line are still likely to suffer from severe deprivation and face the risk of dying prematurely from poverty-related causes. Our understanding of the magnitude of poverty also changes significantly if a higher poverty line is used, one that accurately

reflects how much financial income is needed to fulfil the right to 'a standard of living adequate for... health and well-being' (Universal Declaration of Human Rights, Article 25.1). More than 40 percent of humanity live on less than $5.50 a day, for example, including some 90 percent of the population in South Asia and sub-Saharan Africa. A multidimensional view of poverty—wherein other aspects of deprivation are included, such as access to healthcare, basic utilities, education and security—reveals an alarming truth: that the vast majority of all people in the developing world lack sufficient means to live a healthy and dignified life. At the time of writing in 2021, the World Bank admits that, even by its own measures, global extreme poverty is expected to rise by a further 150 million people due to Covid-19 and its disastrous economic consequences. The first of the Sustainable Development Goals—to bring the global absolute poverty rate to less than 3 percent by 2030—is now considered beyond reach 'without swift, significant, and substantial policy action'.

11 When these words were originally written, such regional uprisings and protest movements were a highly prominent feature in world affairs. Anti-austerity mobilisations were particularly vibrant and ongoing in countries such as Greece, Canada, Germany, England, and also France where the 'Nuit debout' movement had recently emerged.

12 This figure may seem questionably large, but it in fact probably underestimates the amount of people who needlessly die each day as a result of extreme poverty and inadequate social protection. The calculation was originally based on 'Disease burden and mortality estimates' from the World Health Organisation in 2012. Only communicable, maternal, perinatal, and nutritional diseases were considered for the analysis, referred to as 'Group I' causes by the WHO. Ninety six percent of all deaths from

these causes occur in low- and middle-income countries and are considered largely preventable. Yet the true extent of life-threatening deprivation worldwide—largely ignored by the mainstream media—is set to increase considerably as a result of the coronavirus pandemic. At the end of 2020, the United Nations estimated that 270 million people were either at high risk of, or already facing, acute levels of hunger.

13 *Studies on the Principle of Sharing*, op cit.

14 The idea of sharing the world's resources is emerging as a key theme in many areas of progressive policy thinking. For example, central to the UN climate change negotiations is the debate on how all nations can share the limited capacity of the planet's atmosphere to absorb carbon emissions, and in a way that safeguards the economic interests of both developed and developing nations. The concept of 'fair shares' has long been adopted by civil society organisations to frame this debate, which helps to illustrate the need for all people to meet their basic needs without transgressing the planet's environmental limits. Economic sharing is also central to 'cap and share' models for regulating fossil fuel consumption, as well as the widely endorsed 'contraction and convergence' framework for equalising global per capita emissions. Metrics such as the 'ecological footprint' serve to graphically demonstrate how humanity continues to use more resources than the planet can regenerate each year, while failing to share those resources within the constraints of nature's bounds. At the same time, academics and sustainability practitioners have long recognised the need for localised economic alternatives that reflect the concept of 'One planet living', which is concerned with how individuals can enjoy a high quality of life without consuming more than their fair share of finite resources. Proposals for post-growth societies or 'degrowth' can be appraised from this perspective, where the aim

is to reduce material and energy consumption in a socially just manner. Emphasis is therefore placed on a fair distribution of wealth and income, more convivial and participatory societies, and the revivification of the commons. For more background, see: Share The World's Resources, 'Sharing as our Common Cause', December 2014, www.sharing.org/commoncause

15   cf. Mohammed Sofiane Mesbahi, *The intersection of politics and spirituality in addressing the climate crisis*, Matador books, 2016 (see Part II: The inner and outer CO2).

16   In the late 1970s, Willy Brandt (former Chancellor of Germany) convened an Independent Commission of accomplished statesmen and experts to review the 'immense risks threatening mankind'. The final report, entitled North-South: A Programme for Survival, received much publicity and remains one of the best-selling books on international development of all time. Following the Brandt Commission's proposal for an international meeting at the highest level, leaders of eight industrialised and 14 developing nations gathered in Cancun, Mexico, in October 1981 for a summit aimed at breaking the deadlock in years of protracted negotiations on problems of world poverty. The hope was that representative heads of state would meet in an informal setting for two days, thereby creating the momentum and goodwill that would permit global negotiations to advance among all nations. In the end, however, no firm proposals materialised and the demands of Southern countries for a global reallocation of resources remained unmet. US President Ronald Reagan notably rejected the summit's aims to bridge the wealth gap between the few industrialised nations and the majority of poorer countries. While not all of the Brandt Commission's recommendations remain appropriate today (particularly its emphasis on increased trade liberalisation and global Keynesian policies in an era when we are fast approaching environmental limits), there is still much that policymakers and civil society

campaigners can draw from its 'program of priorities' and its vision for a more equitable world. Above all, this includes the proposed five-year Emergency Programme that would necessitate massive resource transfers to less developed countries and far-reaching agrarian reforms. The Commission also called for a new global monetary system, a new approach to development finance, a coordinated process of disarmament, and a global transition away from dependence on non-renewable energy sources. To date, governments have yet to realise Brandt's vision of a multilateral process for 'discussing the entire range of North-South issues among all the nations, with the support and collaboration of the relevant international agencies'. See: Willy Brandt, *North-South: A Programme for Survival* (The Brandt Report), MIT Press, 1980; Willy Brandt, *Common Crisis, North-South: Co-Operation for World Recovery*, The Brandt Commission, London: Pan 1983.

17 For more background, see: Share The World's Resources, 'The United Nations and the principle of sharing', September 2007, www.sharing.org/unitednations

18 For more background, see: 'Financing the global sharing economy', op cit, Part three: Increase international aid, www.sharing.org/financing-report/aid

19 Article 25 of The Universal Declaration of Human Rights states: (1) Everyone has the right to a standard of living adequate for the health and well-being of himself and of his family, including food, clothing, housing and medical care and necessary social services, and the right to security in the event of unemployment, sickness, disability, widowhood, old age or other lack of livelihood in circumstances beyond his control. (2) Motherhood and childhood are entitled to special care and assistance. All children, whether born in or out of wedlock, shall enjoy the same social protection.

20 cf. Financing the global sharing economy, op cit.

21 This perspective and vision is further expanded in our flagship book: *Heralding Article 25: A People's Strategy for World Transformation*, op cit.

22 See note 16.

23 cf. 'The United Nations and the principle of sharing', op cit.

24 Each kingdom in nature grows from the one below it, and a fifth kingdom higher than the human—known as the spiritual kingdom or 'Kingdom of Souls'—has always been with us (as taught by Christ Himself), and is now gradually precipitating on the physical plane. As explained in the writings of Alice A. Bailey, that kingdom is 'composed of all those who down the ages, have sought spiritual goals, liberated themselves from the limitations of the physical body, emotional controls and the obstructive mind. Its citizens are those who today (unknown to the majority) live in physical bodies, work for the welfare of humanity, use love instead of emotion as their general technique, and compose that great body of illumined Minds which guides the destiny of the world.' (*The Externalization of the Hierarchy*, Lucis Press Ltd, 1957).

25 For more on this subject, see: *The intersection of politics and spirituality in addressing the climate crisis: A dialogue with Mohammed Sofiane Mesbahi*, Matador books, 2020.

26 See Annex: The gift economy and barter, page 89

27 See in particular: *Education in the New Age*, Lucis Press Ltd, 1954; *Letters on Occult Meditation*, Letter IX, Lucis Publishing Company, 1922; *The Unfinished Autobiography*, Appendixes, Lucis Publishing Company, 1951.

28 The Ageless Wisdom refers to an ancient body of teachings regarding the energetic structure of the universe, the evolution

of consciousness in man and nature, and the spiritual reality of our lives with an emphasis on right human relations. It has been described as the golden thread that connects the esoteric or hidden teachings that underlie the major religious traditions, while providing the inspiration for the arts and sciences throughout the ages. Although thousands of years old, the teachings are referred to as 'ageless' rather than 'ancient' due to their progressively revelatory nature that is given active expression in people's own lives and experiences. Over the past century, the exoteric form of these teachings have spread widely in the West following their release to the general public by Helena Blavatsky, founder of the Theosophical Society, and later through the works of Annie Besant, Charles Leadbeater, Alice Bailey, Helena Roerich, Rudolf Steiner and Benjamin Creme, among many others.

29 In this context, our conception of 'inner space' can be understood in terms of the time and economic means, as well as the social support and cultivated interest that is necessary for the average person to dedicate themselves to serious practice of the Art of Living. This has immense implications for our present systems of education and the truly universal provision of social protection, as alluded to in the preceding chapters.

30 The Spiritual Hierarchy is the aggregate of those members of humanity who have, through self-mastery, achieved mastery within the whole field of human evolution. Known as the Masters of Wisdom, the senior members of the Hierarchy are the custodians of the Divine Plan for this planet, working from behind the scenes through their disciples in every major field of world work: political, religious, educational, scientific, philosophical, psychological and economic. The outstanding and dramatic feature of Hierarchical action in the present era is the preparation now under way for its return to outer plane activity. The emergence of a new kingdom in nature, the fifth kingdom or

Kingdom of Souls, is precipitating on earth at this time, and will distinguish a new age for humanity as various Ashrams of the Masters are externalised and become publicly known. To learn more about the nature and work of our planetary Hierarchy, see in particular the following works by the Master D.K. written through Alice A. Bailey and published by the Lucis Trust: Initiation, Human and Solar, 1922; The Reappearance of the Christ, 1948; The Externalisation of the Hierarchy, 1957. More contemporary information can also be found in the books by Benjamin Creme published by Share International.

31　For the astute reader who raises eyebrows here, it should be stressed that this is a symbolic and not strictly literal statement. In the Ageless Wisdom teachings, it is Shamballa that represents the head centre of the planet (corresponding to the crown chakra in man). That is the 'Centre where the will of God is known', the highest spiritual centre on earth which embodies the Will and Purpose of our Planetary Logos. There resides the Council of the Lord of the World—the 'Ancient of Days' of the Old Testament, or the First Kumara of the Hindu Scriptures—Who issues forth the Divine Plan of evolution through the agency of the second major centre, the Spiritual Hierarchy (or Kingdom of Souls). This second centre expresses the divine aspect of Love, and is headed by the one we know as Christ, or World Teacher, Who is also the embodiment of the love principle of Deity (the Christ Principle). He is the great human-divine Messenger who seeks to bring about a closer relationship between the Spiritual Hierarchy and the third major centre—humanity as a whole—where the intelligence of God manifests.

Much more can be read of these essential facts in the writings of Alice Bailey and Benjamin Creme in particular, although the observation we are making about the spiritual role and purpose of the United Nations is somewhat different. Christ, we stated, expresses the heart centre (love aspect) of humanity, although it is up to humanity itself to reflect and sustain that love through its coordinated activities on a world level. Thus it may be said that the United Nations is tasked with navigating love to where it belongs, as primarily achieved by supervising a massive logistical operation for rightly sharing planetary resources. In this sense, a vastly expanded and strengthened United Nations organisation may come to express (symbolically speaking) the head centre of humanity, not only in terms of its economic and law-making functions but in every department of its future activity. The esotericist may find it illuminating to reflect upon the immense role of the 7th Ray of Ceremonial Order in building these new forms of world governance over the coming age, in which respect the United Nations of today is still at its most embryonic stage.

32 cf. *Heralding Article 25*, op cit.

33 See note 10.

34 The sentiments in this passage appear more salient in light of the global coronavirus pandemic since early 2020. Despite pleas from low and middle-income countries for the mandatory worldwide sharing of a Covid-19 vaccine, wealthier nations have refused to adequately support a system of fair allocation through the United Nations. Instead, global North governments have conspired with pharmaceutical companies to hoard enough vaccinations to inoculate their populations several times over, leading to a massive shortfall in available doses for the global South. As of writing, the poorest countries have still only received 0.2 percent of the global supply—described as a 'catastrophic moral failure' by the World Health Organisation (WHO). Not a single pharmaceutical company has donated its scientific knowhow to the WHO's technology sharing initiative, while rich countries block all attempts to waive intellectual property rights

on successful vaccines that were largely subsidised by taxpayers. Multilateral responses from the leading industrialised nations have remained grossly inadequate and underfunded, leaving poor countries waiting for charitable donations in the absence of any serious international effort to pool resources and cooperate in a spirit of mutual solidarity. In short, the failure of governments to deliver vaccines as a global public good—available for all people, everywhere, free of charge—has only served to underscore the very lack of the existence of a sharing economy, and the very lack of compassion that defines technological innovation where profit is given primacy over human life.

35 See note 30.

36 See the Annex for further observations on this theme.

37 It should be noted that these words were written when Barack Obama was still in the White House. As the first African American president of the United States, his candidacy in 2008 raised more money than any previous election and saw a historic voter turnout. The great hopes for his premiership were reflected in a Nobel Peace Prize award less than a year later, which cited Obama's assurances of nuclear non-proliferation and a new climate in international relations, especially in light of the previous administration's 'War on Terror'. After two terms in office, however, Obama's foreign policy had only expanded America's global hegemony with, for example, record military spending post-World War II; devastating bombing campaigns in Iraq, Syria, Afghanistan, Pakistan, Libya, Somalia and Yemen; the militarisation of the Baltic states and Eastern Europe; and a trillion dollar increase in nuclear weaponry that violated UN resolutions.

38 Mohammed Sofiane Mesbahi, *The Commons of Humanity*, Matador books, forthcoming in 2022.

About the author

Mohammed Sofiane Mesbahi is the founder of Share The World's Resources (STWR), a civil society organisation based in London, UK, with consultative status at the Economic and Social Council of the United Nations. STWR is a not-for-profit organisation registered in England, no. 4854864.

Editorial assistance: Adam W. Parsons.

9 781803 130583